Joomla! 1.5 Templates Cookbook

Over 60 simple but incredibly effective recipes for taking control of Joomla! templates

Richard Carter

BIRMINGHAM - MUMBAI

Joomla! 1.5 Templates Cookbook

First published: July 2010

Production Reference: 1290610

Published by Packt Publishing Ltd.
32 Lincoln Road
Olton
Birmingham, B27 6PA, UK.

ISBN 978-1-849511-24-7

www.packtpub.com

Cover Image by Javier Barria (Javier.Barria@cwpanama.com)

Credits

Author

Richard Carter

Reviewers

Jose Argudo Blanco

Ryan Bishop

Peter Martin

Oleg Nesterov

Acquisition Editor

Sarah Cullington

Development Editor

Swapna Verlekar

Technical Editor

Namita Sahni

Indexer

Hemangini Bari

Editorial Team Leader

Akshara Aware

Project Team Leader

Lata Basantani

Project Coordinator

Jovita Pinto

Proofreader

Aaron Nash

Production Coordinator

Aparna Bhagat

Cover Work

Aparna Bhagat

About the Author

Richard Carter started as a freelance web designer in Leicestershire, England. He founded his current business, Peacock Carter, in 2006. Currently, he is the senior frontend web developer and a managing director of Peacock Carter Ltd—a web design agency based in the North East of England with specialist knowledge in open source software for business and organizations across the world.

He has worked for clients including Directgov, NHS Choices, and BusinessLink.gov.uk. He tweets from `twitter.com/RichardCarter` and blogs at `earlgreyandbattenburg.co.uk`.

Richard is the author of *MediaWiki Skins Design* and *Magento 1.3 Theme Design*, and has also reviewed *MediaWiki 1.1 Beginner's Guide*.

I'd like to thank Michael, my business partner, for keeping the business running while I was busy writing and researching the book. A brief "hello" and thanks is also due to Alex, EJ, and Joy.

About the Reviewers

Jose Argudo Blanco is a web developer from Valencia, Spain. After finishing his studies, he started working for a web design company. Then, six years later, he decided to start working as a freelancer.

Now that some years have passed as a freelancer, he thinks it's the best decision he has ever taken, a decision that let him work with the tools he likes, such as Joomla!, CodeIgniter, CakePHP, jQuery, and other known open source technologies.

His desire to learn and share his knowledge has led him to be a regular reviewer of books, such as *Wordpress 2.8 Theme Design*, *Joomla! With Flash*, *Joomla! 1.5 SEO*, *Magento Theme Design*, and *Symfony 1.3 Web Application Development* from Packt.

Recently, he has even published his own book, *CodeIgniter 1.7*, which you can also find at Packt's site. If you work with PHP, take a look at it!

Now he's working on a new book for Packt—this time it's Joomla! related. Check it out soon!

If you want to know more about him, you can check his site `www.joseargudo.com`.

To Silvia, she's the best thing that has happened to me.

Ryan Bishop is a 27-year-old freelance web designer specializing in CMS templates and themes for open source content management systems. He's the former proprietor of Art Star Design LLC—a small web design company focused on CMS-powered small business websites.

I'd like to thank my parents, Gene and Linda Bishop, for their endless support and love.

Peter Martin has a keen interest in computers, programming, sharing knowledge, and how people (mis)use information technology. He has a Bachelor's degree in Economics (International Marketing Management) and a Master's degree in Mass Communication. He discovered PHP/MySQL in 2003 and Joomla!'s predecessor, Mambo CMS, a year later. Peter has his own business `www.db8.nl` (founded in 2005) and he supports companies and organizations with Joomla! and Joomla! extension development.

Peter is actively involved in the Joomla! community where he is a member of the Community Leadership Team and Global Moderator at Joomla! forum.

His other interests are JCI (Junior Chamber International) Netherlands where he is currently Project Manager Internet. He loves open source software, Ubuntu Linux, music (vinyl records), and art house movies. Peter lives in Nijmegen, the Netherlands.

Oleg Nesterov is a professional web developer. He holds a Master's degree in Mechanics and Mathematics (diploma with honors) from Sumy State University in Ukraine. Since graduation he has figured out the three main principles for his life: having a mission, loving what you do, and constant self-development. He tries to follow each of these principles in his life and job. That's why he's a web developer.

He enjoys sharing his experience with others, teaching people, and creating tools that increase developers' productivity. He spends his spare time working.

Oleg runs mindK lab (`http://www.mindk-lab.com`), a web development company, which focuses on producing custom Joomla! extensions, templates, and websites of the highest quality.

Table of Contents

Preface

With the widespread empowering of website owners being able to manage their own website's content, there are a huge number of content management systems available. Joomla! is one of the most popular of these content management systems with a large user base and active community who are constantly working to improve Joomla! for new and future users.

With the popularity of Joomla! and the relative lack of customized templates, there is much that can be done to change the appearance of your Joomla! website—from customizing the administration panel to creating print-friendly views of your website content and integrating popular applications such as Twitter and Facebook into your Joomla! website.

What this book covers

Chapter 1, Joomla! Theming Basics, covers changing the basics of your Joomla! templates, from the color scheme using template variations to your site's logo, and using the administration panel to edit your template's HTML and CSS.

Chapter 2, Custom Joomla! Templates, goes through more detailed templating tasks, from using CSS resets with your template to providing a guide to `jdoc` statements in your Joomla! templates.

Chapter 3, Theming the Details, covers styling search forms at both module and component view to pagination and beyond.

Chapter 4, Custom Page Templates, contains guides on creating custom error and site offline pages, and a walkthrough to module chrome.

Chapter 5, Styling Joomla! for Print, covers everything to do with print stylesheets, from typography to layout and troubleshooting common bugs in print CSS.

Chapter 6, Joomla! Admin Templates, contains guides to customizing Joomla!'s administration panel, from installing a new admin template to changing the admin panel's colors.

Chapter 7, Social Media and Joomla!, covers guides to integrating social media content such as videos from YouTube and content from Twitter into your Joomla! templates.

Chapter 8, Styling Joomla! for Mobiles, provides guides to styling your Joomla! website for mobile devices such as the iPhone, from creating handheld devices stylesheets in CSS to adding iPhone icons for your website.

Chapter 9, Joomla! and JavaScript, includes tips on minimizing page load time when using JavaScript in your Joomla! template and integrating Lightbox and other JavaScript features into your template.

Chapter 10, Miscellaneous Joomla! Templating, includes a miscellany of content for Joomla! template designers, from using conditional comments only for Internet Explorer CSS fixes to fixing Firefox/Mozilla bugs and more.

Appendix, Joomla! Output Overrides, covers the use of template overrides in Joomla!.

What you need for this book

You'll need Joomla! 1.5 installed either locally or on a server you have access to. For more information on Joomla!'s requirements, visit `http://www.joomla.org/technical-requirements.html`.

Who this book is for

This book is written for Joomla! developers who want to improve the look and feel of their Joomla! sites. Readers are expected to have knowledge of CSS and (X)HTML. And although knowledge of Joomla! theming will be helpful, it is not required.

Conventions

In this book, you will find a number of styles of text that distinguish between different kinds of information. Here are some examples of these styles and an explanation of their meaning.

Code words in text are shown as follows: "Access your Joomla! website via FTP and navigate to the `templates` directory."

A block of code is set as follows:

```
#search input[type='text']:focus {
border-color: #09C /* blue */
}
```

When we wish to draw your attention to a particular part of a code block, the relevant lines or items are set in bold:

```html
<span class="pagination">

  <span>&laquo;</span>
  <span>Start</span>
  <span>Prev</span><strong>
  <span>1</span></strong>
```

New terms and **important words** are shown in bold. Words that you see on the screen, in menus or dialog boxes for example, appear in the text like this: "Select the file from your computer and then click on the **Upload File & Install** button."

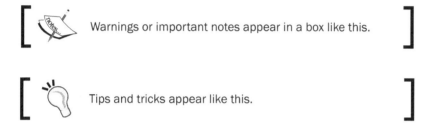

> Warnings or important notes appear in a box like this.

> Tips and tricks appear like this.

Reader feedback

Feedback from our readers is always welcome. Let us know what you think about this book—what you liked or may have disliked. Reader feedback is important for us to develop titles that you really get the most out of.

To send us general feedback, simply send an e-mail to feedback@packtpub.com, and mention the book title via the subject of your message.

If there is a book that you need and would like to see us publish, please send us a note in the **SUGGEST A TITLE** form on www.packtpub.com or e-mail suggest@packtpub.com.

If there is a topic that you have expertise in and you are interested in either writing or contributing to a book on, see our author guide on www.packtpub.com/authors.

Customer support

Now that you are the proud owner of a Packt book, we have a number of things to help you to get the most from your purchase.

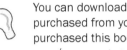

Downloading the example code for this book

You can download the example code files for all Packt books you have purchased from your account at http://www.PacktPub.com. If you purchased this book elsewhere, you can visit http://www.PacktPub.com/support and register to have the files emailed directly to you.

Errata

Although we have taken every care to ensure the accuracy of our content, mistakes do happen. If you find a mistake in one of our books—maybe a mistake in the text or the code—we would be grateful if you would report this to us. By doing so, you can save other readers from frustration and help us improve subsequent versions of this book. If you find any errata, please report them by visiting http://www.packtpub.com/support, selecting your book, clicking on the **let us know** link, and entering the details of your errata. Once your errata are verified, your submission will be accepted and the errata will be uploaded on our website, or added to any list of existing errata, under the Errata section of that title. Any existing errata can be viewed by selecting your title from http://www.packtpub.com/support.

Piracy

Piracy of copyright material on the Internet is an ongoing problem across all media. At Packt, we take the protection of our copyright and licenses very seriously. If you come across any illegal copies of our works, in any form, on the Internet, please provide us with the location address or website name immediately so that we can pursue a remedy.

Please contact us at copyright@packtpub.com with a link to the suspected pirated material.

We appreciate your help in protecting our authors and our ability to bring you valuable content.

Questions

You can contact us at questions@packtpub.com if you are having a problem with any aspect of the book, and we will do our best to address it.

1
Joomla! Theming Basics

In this chapter, we will cover the basics of theming our Joomla! website:

- ▶ Finding the current default template
- ▶ Locating Joomla! templates in your website's hierarchy
- ▶ Understanding Joomla! templates
- ▶ Changing your template's color variation
- ▶ Adding a color variation
- ▶ Changing your template's logo
- ▶ Selecting the default Joomla! template
- ▶ Editing the HTML template in the administration panel
- ▶ Editing CSS in the administration panel

Introduction

In this chapter, you'll cover the basics of changing your Joomla! template, from finding the location of the default Joomla! template to changing your website's logo and altering your template's color scheme.

Finding the current default template

Our first task is to discover which Joomla! template our website is using.

Getting ready

Log in to the Joomla! administration panel, which you can reach by going to the `http://www.example.com/administrator` directory (where Joomla! is installed) in your web browser.

How to do it...

1. Once logged in to your Joomla! website's administration panel, navigate to the **Template Manager** feature under **Extensions | Template Manager** in the menu.

2. Once the page has loaded, you will see a list of the templates that are currently installed on your Joomla!-powered website.

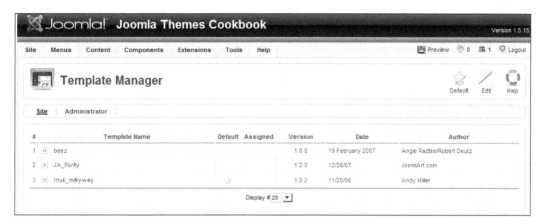

3. The current default template displays a star icon under the **Default** title in the table, so the template that is the current default on your website is called **rhuk_milkyway**, which is installed by default.

How it works...

Joomla!'s **Template Manager** feature in the administration panel allows you to see which templates are currently installed. It also allows you to change which template is the current default that your website's visitors will see.

There's more...

You can view more information on a template by clicking on the name of the template in the administration panel's **Template Manager** section.

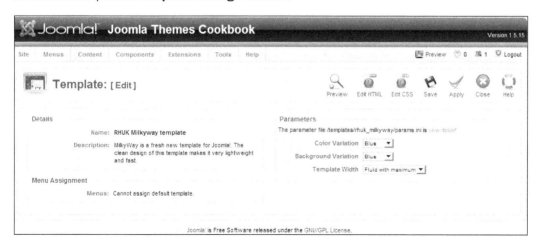

If you hover over the name of the template in the list, you'll see a small thumbnail preview of what the Joomla! template looks like: it can be useful picking a new default template for your website.

See also

▸ *Finding the current default template*

▸ *Locating Joomla! templates in your website's hierarchy*

▸ *Understanding Joomla! templates*

▸ *Changing your template's logo*

Locating Joomla! templates in your website's hierarchy

When building your Joomla! template it's useful to know where in Joomla! the files for each template are stored within your website's hierarchy.

Getting ready

Open your FTP program if your Joomla! website is stored on a remote server and locate the root directory of your Joomla! installation. Let's assume that our Joomla! installation is on `example.com` and that we're using FTP throughout the book. We'll use **FileZilla**, which can be downloaded for free from `http://filezilla-project.org`.

How to do it...

1. Locate the directory where your Joomla! is installed. Joomla! templates are stored in the `templates` directory. We're looking for the default template we identified previously, *rhuk_milkyway*, which is located in the `rhuk_milkyway` directory:

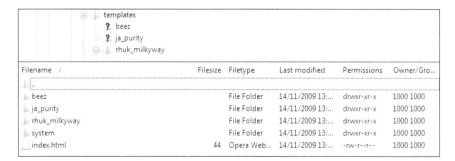

How it works...

By storing related files such as CSS files, images, and the template files together in a Joomla! template, it's easier to see which files relate to a particular Joomla! template.

See also

You may find these other recipes helpful:

- *Understanding Joomla! templates*
- *Installing a Joomla! template*

Understanding Joomla! templates

If you have some experience with theming other content management systems, this can be a good start for learning Joomla! template design. As with theming any content management system, Joomla! does have its quirks and it's useful to look at the structure of a Joomla! template.

Getting ready

View your Joomla! website's files in an FTP program.

How to do it...

If you now view the contents of the `templates\rhuk_milkyway` directory, you can see what a Joomla! template is composed of:

Filename	Filesize	Filetype	Last modified	Permissions	Owner/Gro...
...					
css		File Folder	14/11/2009 13:...	drwxr-xr-x	1000 1000
html		File Folder	14/11/2009 13:...	drwxr-xr-x	1000 1000
images		File Folder	14/11/2009 13:...	drwxr-xr-x	1000 1000
component.php	1,276	PHP File	14/11/2009 13:...	-rw-r--r--	1000 1000
favicon.ico	1,150	Icon	14/11/2009 13:...	-rw-r--r--	1000 1000
index.html	44	Opera Web...	14/11/2009 13:...	-rw-r--r--	1000 1000
index.php	5,615	PHP File	14/11/2009 13:...	-rw-r--r--	1000 1000
params.ini	61	Configurat...	14/11/2009 13:...	-rw-r--r--	1000 1000
template_thumbnail.png	8,001	PNG File	14/11/2009 13:...	-rw-r--r--	1000 1000
templateDetails.xml	4,166	XML Docu...	14/11/2009 13:...	-rw-r--r--	1000 1000

(Folder tree: templates → beez, ja_purity, rhuk_milkyway)

As you can see in the preceding screenshot, there are three directories, which are used in the following ways:

▶ The css directory contains the CSS files

▶ The html directory (which we can ignore for now) contains template overrides for various components and modules if they differ from the default templates provided by that module or component

▶ The images directory contains images associated with the template

There are also a few other files which you'll find useful in building and customizing Joomla! templates:

▶ The favicon.ico file or the 'favorites icon' displays a small icon next to your website's address in the address bar of the visitors' browsers.

▶ The index.php file outputs the (X)HTML of your template.

▶ params.ini defines the color and other variations in your Joomla! template (this file is optional).

▶ template_thumbnail.png provides a screenshot preview of the template that is displayed in Joomla!'s administration panel.

▶ templateDetails.xml provides information about the template itself, such as the designer, the designer's own website address, and any notes the author of the template may have for its users. This file is incredibly important as it is required to be able to allow the template to be installable via the standard Joomla! installation process.

How it works...

When a template is enabled, Joomla! looks for certain files in the template's directory. It looks for the index.php file to generate each page's HTML, which may then reference CSS and other style files. By convention, the CSS files and images referenced in the template's index.php file of a Joomla! theme are stored in subdirectories of the template's main directory.

See also

▶ *Understanding the templateDetails.xml file*

Changing your template's color variation

Some Joomla! templates allow you to change some of their aspects from the administration panel.

Getting ready

Log in to your Joomla! website's administration panel and select **Extensions | Template Manager**. From there, select the *rhuk_milkyway* template, which you'll find has been installed and enabled by default for your Joomla! website. (If you're stuck, view the recipe for *Finding the current default Joomla! template*.)

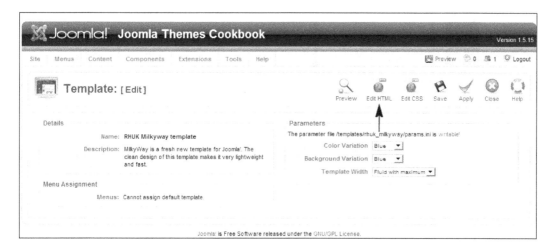

How to do it...

1. Under the **Parameters** section of the template's detailed view, you will see that the *rhuk_milkyway* template has three options to change:

   - The foreground color scheme
   - The background color scheme
   - The width of your pages

By default, with the parameters set to **Blue**, your Joomla! website looks like this—the background color of the page turns to blue, as do the color of headings and the panels surrounding the modules in the left-hand column.

2. Let's select **Red** in the **Parameters** section of the administration page in Joomla!'s **Template Manager** area as the value for the template's **Color Variation** and **Background Variation** values and select the **Save** or **Apply** button to the top-right of the screen. After refreshing your website you should now see that the colors have changed. In particular, the color of the background, headings, and links would have changed.

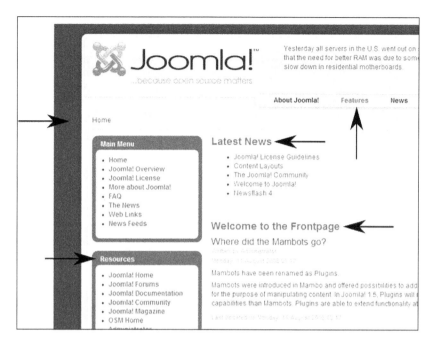

How it works...

Changing these values alters the theme's `params.ini` file, which affects how a theme is displayed by loading additional CSS files in the `<head>` element of your Joomla! template.

The range of values for each parameter is defined in the template's `templateDetails.xml` file. The values that can be selected will vary by template.

There's more...

You may need to make a change to the file permissions to allow these changes to be made from the Joomla! administration panel.

Making the templates\rhuk_milkyway\params.ini file writable

You may find that you are unable to change these values if you see a message that reads **The parameter file /templates/rhuk_milkyway/params.ini is unwritable!**:

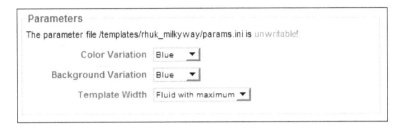

To rectify this problem so that you are able to change the template's parameters, open the `\templates\rhuk_milkyway\` directory in your FTP program. You should then be able to right-click on the `params.ini` file and see a **File Permissions** option in most FTP programs.

You shouldn't have trouble with file permissions on the Windows operating system. For more information on file permissions, see this article on Wikipedia: `http://en.wikipedia.org/wiki/Filesystem_permissions`.

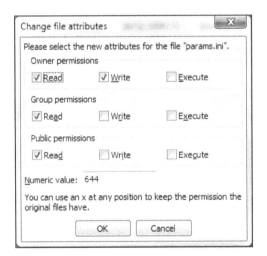

Ensure that the **Group** and **Public** write permissions are checked to allow Joomla! to change this file. Alternatively, you can change the numeric value to **666**, which is the numerical representation of the permissions we need:

See also

▸ *Understanding the templateDetails.xml file.*

▸ *Understanding Joomla! templates*

Adding a color variation

You are not restricted to the color variations provided with a Joomla! template; you can add your own color variations to suit.

To match our website's new logo, we'll be creating a pink/purple color variation of the *rhuk_milkyway* template, though this technique can be adapted for other Joomla! themes that offer color variation options too!

Getting ready

We'll need the hexadecimal color references for our new color variation, taken from the logo file that we'll add to the template in another recipe. These are:

▸ `#D400AA` for pink

▸ `#660080` for purple

We'll be calling our new color variation "pink".

How to do it...

There are three major stages to creating a color variation of a Joomla! template. Firstly, CSS is required. Secondly, any images that need to change with the variation are also required. Then, to make the color variation visible in our administration panel, we need to edit the `templateDetails.xml` file.

1. In the `templates\rhuk_milkyway\css\` directory, create a CSS file named `pink.css`. This file will overwrite the foreground colors for the Joomla! template that you're using:

```
a:link, a:visited {
    color: #D400AA /* pink */
}

a:hover {
    color: #660080; /* purple */
}

#pillmenu a:hover {
  color: #D400AA;
}

#pillmenu a#active_menu-nav {
  background: url(../images/pink/mw_menu_active_bg.png) 0 0
  repeat-x;
  color: #fff;
}

#pillmenu a#active_menu-nav:hover {
  color: #fff;
}

h3, .componentheading, table.moduletable th {
  color: #D400AA;
}

div.module_menu {
    background: url(../images/pink/mw_box_br.png) 100% 100%
    no-repeat;
}
```

```
div.module_menu div {
    background: url(../images/pink/mw_box_bl.png) 0 100% no-repeat;
}

div.module_menu div div {
    background: url(../images/pink/mw_box_tr.png) 100% 0 no-repeat;
}

div.module_menu div div div {
    background: url(../images/pink/mw_box_tl.png) 0 0 no-repeat;
}
```

2. If you want the background colors to change too, you'll need to create another CSS file in this directory called `pink_bg.css`:

```
#page_bg {
    background: #660080;
}

div#wrapper {
  background: #f7f7f7 url(../images/pink/mw_shadow_l.png) 0 0
  repeat-y;
}

div#wrapper_r {
    background: url(../images/pink/mw_shadow_r.png) 100% 0 repeat-y;
}

div#header {
    background: url(../images/pink/mw_header_t.png) 0 0 repeat-x;
}

div#header_l {
    background: url(../images/pink/mw_header_t_l.png) 0 0
    no-repeat;
}

div#header_r {
    background: url(../images/pink/mw_header_t_r.png) 100% 0
    no-repeat;
}
```

```
div#footer {
  background: #f7f7f7 url(../images/pink/mw_footer_b.png) 0 100%
  repeat-x;
}

div#footer_l {
    background: url(../images/pink/mw_footer_b_l.png) 0 0
    no-repeat;
}

div#footer_r {
    background: url(../images/pink/mw_footer_b_r.png) 100% 0
    no-repeat;
}
```

From the CSS, you may have noticed that a large number of image files are referenced, which provide the corners within the template's design, and a color-coordinated image that appears when you hover over an item in the navigation menu of your website.

3. In the `templates\rhuk_milkyway\images\` directory, copy and paste the images from one color variation (for example, black) to create a new directory, and name it pink.

    These images now need recreating, aliased to our new background colors. Luckily for you, they should be included in the code download provided with the book!

    To ensure that the new color variation is detected by Joomla!'s administration panel, you now need to edit the `templateDetails.xml` file in `templates\rhuk_milkyway\`.

4. Locate the code in `templateDetails.xml` that begins with `<param>`:

```
<param name="colorVariation" type="list" default="white"
       label="Color Variation"
       description="Color variation to use">
  <option value="blue">Blue</option>
  <option value="red">Red</option>
  <option value="green">Green</option>
  <option value="orange">Orange</option>
  <option value="black">Black</option>
  <option value="white">White</option>
</param>
```

5. Here, you need to add an option for your new pink color variation:

```
<param name="colorVariation" type="list" default="white"
        label="Color Variation"
        description="Color variation to use">
   <option value="blue">Blue</option>
   <option value="pink">Pink</option>
   <option value="red">Red</option>
   <option value="green">Green</option>
   <option value="orange">Orange</option>
   <option value="black">Black</option>
   <option value="white">White</option>
</param>
```

Beneath this code, you also need an option to be able to change the template's background color scheme to your new pink variation:

```
<param name="backgroundVariation" type="list" default="blue"
        label="Background Variation"
        description="Background color variation to use">
   <option value="blue">Blue</option>
   <option value="pink">Pink</option>
   <option value="red">Red</option>
   <option value="green">Green</option>
   <option value="orange">Orange</option>
   <option value="black">Black</option>
   <option value="white">White</option>
</param>
```

6. Save and upload the `templateDetails.xml` file to your server.

7. Now all you need to do is change the template's color variation in the **Parameters** area of the template's settings screen in your Joomla! website's administration panel. Select the **Pink** option for both the **Color Variation** and **Background Variation** values and click on **Apply**. Refresh the page and you should see the new color variation on your Joomla! theme:

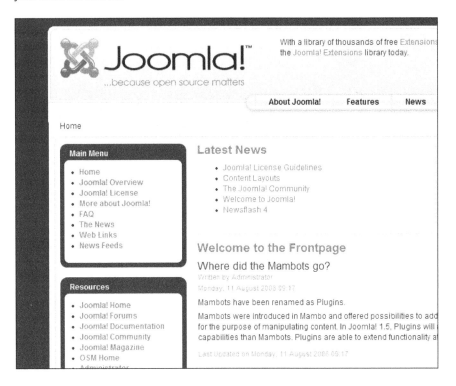

If you need help doing this, see the *Changing your template's color variation* section of this chapter.

How it works...

After setting the color variation parameters for the template, when Joomla! loads a page for a visitor it also loads additional CSS files that overwrite particular references for colors throughout the theme.

See also

- ▸ *Changing your template's color variation*
- ▸ *Changing your template's logo*

Changing your template's logo

One of the most fundamental changes that you will want to make to your Joomla! template is to change the logo.

Getting ready

You will find the logo of rhuk_milkyway in the `templates\rhuk_milkyway\images` directory of your Joomla! website's installation. The file that we're looking for is called `mw_joomla_logo.png`.

How to do it...

1. Save the logo file as `mw_joomla_logo.png`. You'll be using this logo for your Joomla! website:

    jtheme**designer**

2. Upload the new logo file from your computer to the template's `image` directory. Refresh your website and you should see your new logo display:

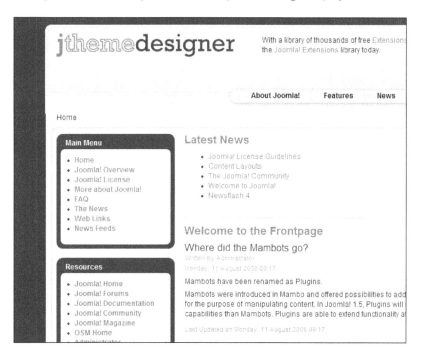

You may find it helpful to save a backup copy of the default logo, just in case!

Can't see the new logo? If you don't see the new logo, you may need to delete your browser's cache.

How it works...

By overwriting the default logo file for your Joomla! template, you can quickly and relatively easily start customizing your website for your own needs.

See also

▸ *Changing your template's color variation*

Selecting the default Joomla! template

You can select the default Joomla! template to be displayed on your website from the administration panel.

Getting ready

Log in to the administration panel and navigate to the **Template Manager** feature (available from the **Extensions | Template Manager** option in the menu).

How to do it...

1. Select the radio button next to the theme's name; we'll select the *JA_Purity* template for this example.

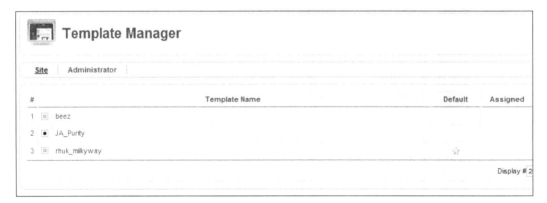

2. Click on the **Default** button to select that template as the default template displayed on your website:

3. Refresh the frontend of your website, and you'll see the new template in action:

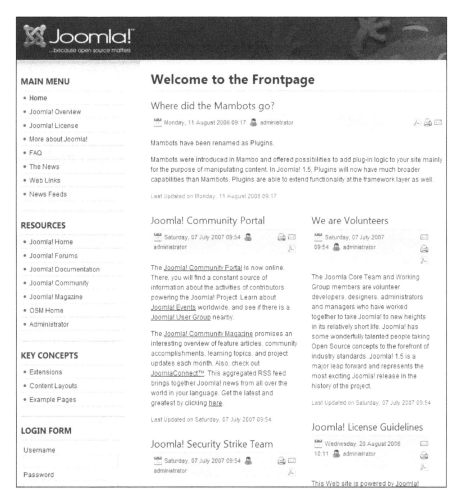

Notice that the content remains the same, but the design changes. For the purposes of this book, we'll now revert the default template to *rhuk_milkyway*.

How it works...

By selecting a new template as the default, you can change Joomla!'s look and feel quite substantially.

See also

▸ *Changing your template's logo*

▸ *Changing your template's color variation*

Editing the HTML template in the administration panel

Joomla! allows administrators of their website to edit HTML templates of their Joomla! templates within the administration panel.

Getting ready

Log in to your website's administration panel and navigate to the **Template Manager** feature. From here, select the theme that is the current default. For this example, we'll assume it's the *rhuk_milkyway* template:

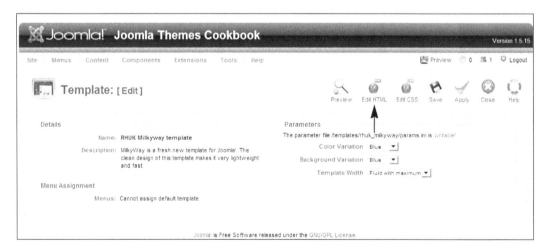

How to do it...

1. Select the **Edit HTML** option at the top-right of your screen. You'll be presented with a text box containing the contents of the template's `index.php` file:

2. Once you have finished editing the file, click on **Save** or **Apply**, or simply click on **Cancel** to preserve the template file as it was.

   Being able to edit a template's HTML from the administration panel is convenient for smaller tasks. For example, what if we wanted to remove the text at the bottom of the website that reads **Powered by Joomla!**?

   Powered by Joomla!. valid XHTML and CSS.

3. Now locate the code that reads as follows:

```
<p id="power_by">
  <?php echo JText::_('Powered by') ?>
  <a href="http://www.joomla.org">Joomla!</a>.
  <?php echo JText::_('Valid') ?>
  <a href="http://validator.w3.org/check/referer">XHTML</a>
  <?php echo JText::_('and') ?>
  <a href="http://jigsaw.w3.org/css-validator/check/referer">CSS
  </a>.
</p>
```

By removing the highlighted lines of code in the previous code snippet, we can remove reference to the website being powered by Joomla!, if we wish to. Depending on the template you're editing, this process will almost certainly vary.

4. Once the **Save** or **Apply** button has been clicked, refresh the frontend of your website (that is, not the administration panel):

How it works...

When you edit the HTML of your template in Joomla!'s administration panel, Joomla! overwrites the `index.php` of your template with the changes that you've made. If you have downloaded your template for editing, you will need to download the `index.php` file again to prevent overwriting any changes.

See also

  ▸ *Editing CSS in the administration panel*

Editing CSS in the administration panel

Joomla! also allows administrators of their website to edit the CSS files associated with their Joomla! templates from the administration panel.

Getting ready

Navigate to the **Template Manager** feature in the administration panel. From here, select the theme that is currently the default. For this example, we'll assume it's the _rhuk_milkyway_ template again.

How to do it...

1. Select the **Edit CSS** option at the top-right of your screen. You'll be presented with a list of the CSS files associated with the current template:

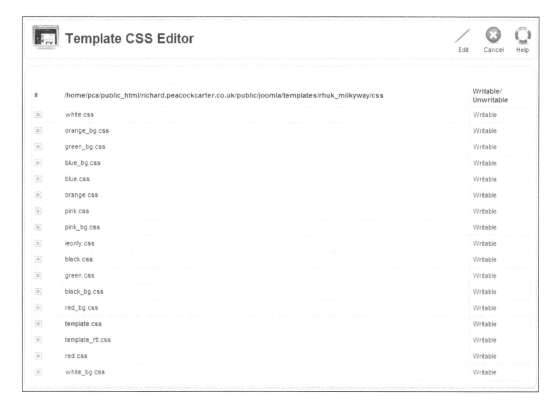

#	/home/pca/public_html/richard.peacockcarter.co.uk/public/joomla/templates/rhuk_milkyway/css	Writable/ Unwritable
○	white.css	Writable
○	orange_bg.css	Writable
○	green_bg.css	Writable
○	blue_bg.css	Writable
○	blue.css	Writable
○	orange.css	Writable
○	pink.css	Writable
○	pink_bg.css	Writable
○	ieonly.css	Writable
○	black.css	Writable
○	green.css	Writable
○	black_bg.css	Writable
○	red_bg.css	Writable
○	template.css	Writable
○	template_rtl.css	Writable
○	red.css	Writable
○	white_bg.css	Writable

2. Select a CSS file by selecting the radio button next to the CSS file's name, and click on the **Edit** button at the top-right of the screen. You will then be presented with the CSS to edit:

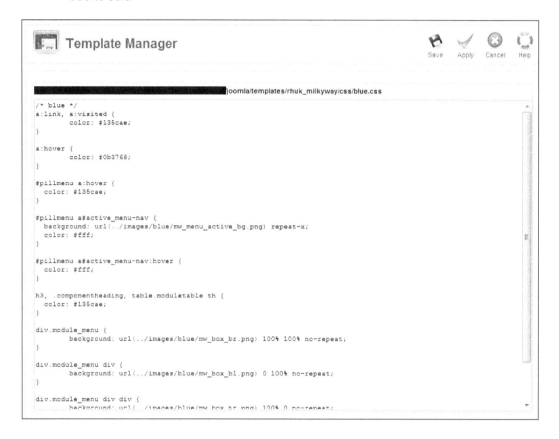

3. Once you have finished editing, click on **Save** or **Apply** or simply click on **Cancel** to negate any changes that you've made to the file.

How it works...

When you edit a CSS file from your Joomla! template in the administration panel, Joomla! overwrites the relevant CSS file with the changes that you've made, so long as the file is writable.

There's more...

There is one common problem that you may face when trying to edit your template's CSS files via the administration panel. You may find that the CSS files for your template are not writable from the administration panel.

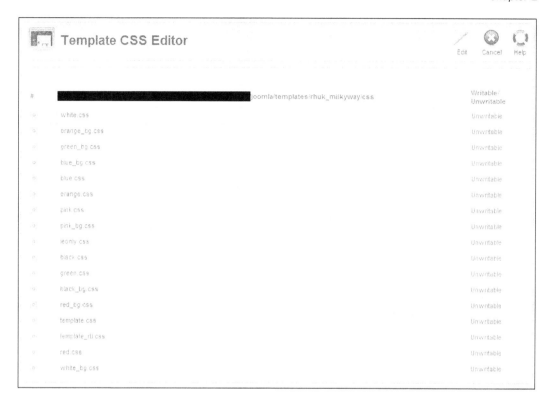

To rectify this problem, navigate to the `\templates\rhuk_milkyway\css` directory where you have Joomla! installed. Select all of the CSS files you wish to be able to edit from the administration panel, right-click, and select **File permissions**:

When changing the permissions to allow access to the template's `params.ini` file, you need to allow **Write** permission for **Group** and **Public**:

Don't allow execution for security

Generally, it's wise to prevent execution of files unless explicitly required, as this can prevent a security risk to your Joomla! website.

Once you refresh the page in the administration panel you should now be able to edit the CSS files associated with the template.

See also

▶   *Editing the HTML template in the administration panel*

2
Custom Joomla! Templates

This chapter includes more customization of Joomla! templates, including:

- ▶ Installing a Joomla! template
- ▶ Understanding Joomla! template positions
- ▶ Understanding `jdoc` statements
- ▶ Understanding the `templateDetails.xml` file
- ▶ Styling for `component.php`
- ▶ Adding a custom favicon to your template
- ▶ Styling Joomla! error messages
- ▶ Styling Joomla! error pages

Introduction

We'll cover the more challenging aspects of editing the template of your Joomla! website in this chapter, from getting to grips with inserting content into your website to adding a multilingual aspect to your website.

Installing a Joomla! template

Knowing how to install a Joomla! template is fundamental knowledge for any Joomla! template designer.

Getting ready

Access your Joomla! website via FTP, and navigate to the `templates` directory. Decompress your Joomla! template if it has been compressed. If you're installing a Joomla! template called `ch2-test`, it should be contained within a directory called `ch2-test`.

How to do it...

1. You can also install templates via Joomla!'s **Template Manager** feature, available from the **Extensions | Install/Uninstall** option in the administration panel's menu:

2. From here, locate the compressed (ZIP) folder that contains your Joomla! template from your computer by using the **File Upload** field under the **Upload Package File** option:

It can be useful to make use of separate tabs in your browser—one for the frontend of your website, and one for Joomla!'s administration panel.

3. If you now enable the newly uploaded template as your Joomla! installation's current template in **Extensions | Template Manager**, you should now be able to see the new template displayed.

How it works...

As we've seen before, a template needs particular files to work—at the very least, a `templateDetails.xml` file and an `index.php` file. When installing your template, at least these two files need to be present so that Joomla! can output content to display to your visitors.

There's more...

There are a few other small tasks that you might want to do once you've installed your Joomla! template.

Checking referenced files exist

It's worthwhile to double-check that all of the files referenced in a theme's `templateDetails.xml` file exist on your server where Joomla! is expecting to see them! These files are referenced in the `templateDetails.xml` file between the `<filename>` elements of the XML file. For example, if this section of the `templateDetails.xml` file contains the following code, it is worth checking that these three files exist within the correct directory:

```
<files>
  <filename>index.php</filename>
  <filename>templateDetails.xml</filename>
  <filename>template_thumbnail.png</filename>
</files>
```

However, some templates comprise hundreds of different files, so it can be difficult to do this!

Reassigning content permissions

Depending on your current Joomla! website's configuration, you may also find that you will need to reassign a module and components to module positions so that they appear!

Installing via FTP

To install a Joomla! template with FTP, upload the files onto your Joomla! website into the `templates\ch2-test` directory. Enable the new template in your website's administration panel (under **Extensions | Template Manager**), and refresh the frontend of your Joomla! website (that is, `example.com` rather than `example.com/administrator`).

See also

> ▸ *Selecting the default Joomla! template*

> ▸ *Understanding Joomla! templates*

Understanding Joomla! template positions

Positions within Joomla! templates let you customize where you can place modules and content in your Joomla!-powered website.

Getting ready

While you're reading this, we'll need the *rhuk_milkyway* template enabled, as this has quite a large number of options for positions within its template.

How to do it...

1. View your Joomla! template in a web browser:

2. Edit the address of the page you're currently on, adding `?tp=1` to the end of it:

3. If you now refresh the page, you'll see the template positions of the various content blocks on your website:

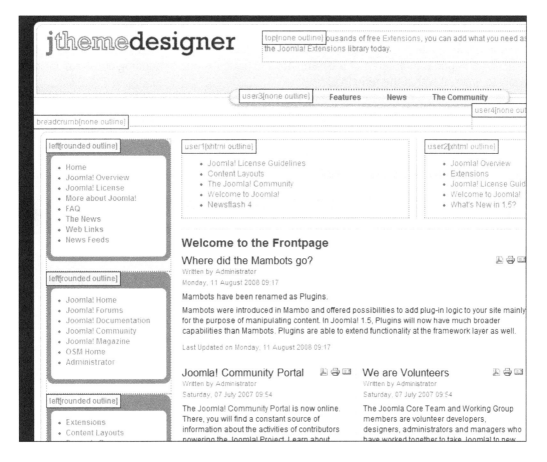

You can see the template positions in boxes at the top-left of each of the blocks of content within the website (for example, **top[none outline], user3[none outline]**).

How it works...

The `?tp=1` addition to the end of the address in your browser tells Joomla! to display information about the template positions, which makes it easy for us to see what Joomla! is doing. The extra information that Joomla! includes in brackets after that gives us additional information on what's happening in the template, which we don't need for now.

Does your URL already contain parameters?

If the end of the address of your Joomla! website already contains parameters (also known as query strings), for example, it looks like `http://example.com/index.php?option=com_content&view=article&id=25&Itemid=28`, then all you need to do is append `&tp=1` to the end, like so: `http://example.com/index.php?option=com_content&view=article&id=25&Itemid=28&tp=1`.

There's more...

Sometimes, template positions can be misleading. Something assigned to the `left` template position can appear in an area of the template you don't expect, depending on where Joomla! is told to insert it within the template.

See also

- *Understanding the templateDetails.xml file*
- *Installing a Joomla! template*

Understanding jdoc statements

Any Joomla! template will need to insert content managed by Joomla! into your website. This is done with the `jdoc` statements in the Joomla! template.

Getting ready

Open the `index.php` file of the *rhuk_milkyway* template, which is located in the `templates\rhuk_milkyway` directory of your Joomla! installation.

How to do it...

Each "block" of content within Joomla! is inserted with a different `jdoc` statement within the `index.php` file. There are four fundamental statements that we'll look at:

- Component `jdoc` statements
- Head `jdoc` statements
- `Module` and `modules` statements

Component jdoc statements

Component `jdoc` statements insert the main content for the current component into your Joomla! template. You can insert the primary page content for a particular page in Joomla! with this `jdoc` statement, within the `<body>` element of your page:

```
<jdoc:include type="component" />
```

Simple! This statement ensures that any page title and content associated with the page is inserted into your template.

Head jdoc statements

The head `jdoc` statement inserts relevant code into the `<head>` element of your page. This includes:

- The current page's title
- The current page's metadata; in particular, the `keywords` and `description` fields for the page
- The `robots` metadata field that tells search engines whether they should take notice of the current page or not
- Links to your template's **favicon** (the icon that appears near the address bar in your browser)
- Links to alternate feeds for your content (that is, RSS and Atom feeds)

```
<jdoc:include type="head" />
```

Typically, this produces code similar to the following code snippet in your template:

```html
<head>
  <meta http-equiv="content-type"
        content="text/html; charset=utf-8" />
  <meta name="robots" content="index, follow" />
  <meta name="keywords" content="joomla, Joomla" />
  <meta name="description"
        content="Joomla! - the dynamic portal engine and content
                 management system" />
  <meta name="generator"
        content="Joomla! 1.5 - Open Source Content Management" />
  <title>Welcome to the Frontpage</title>
  <link href="/joomla/index.php?format=feed&amp;type=rss"
        rel="alternate" type="application/rss+xml" title="RSS 2.0" />
  <link href="/joomla/index.php?format=feed&amp;type=atom"
      rel="alternate" type="application/atom+xml" title="Atom 1.0" />
  <!--some code omitted -->
</head>
```

How it works...

When Joomla! loads a page, it uses the `index.php` file to generate the page that is displayed. The `jdoc` statements tell Joomla! where in the (X)HTML document content is required.

There's more...

There are quite a few different types of `jdoc` statements available to Joomla! templates that aren't used very frequently.

Installation jdoc statement

The installation `jdoc` statement is used only in Joomla!'s installer template, so it is not of much use to the frontend Joomla! templates:

```
<jdoc:include type="installation" />
```

Message jdoc statement

The message `jdoc` statement inserts any system messages or error messages that Joomla! needs to display:

```
<jdoc:include type="message" />
```

It may be worth surrounding this in a `<div>` tag made collapsible by using JavaScript so that your visitors can close the message once it has been read.

jdoc statements and the style attribute

If you have looked at other Joomla! template files, you may have come across `jdoc` statements similar to this one:

```
<jdoc:include type="modules" name="top" style="xhtml" />
```

The `style` attribute refers to the **module chrome** so that if no value for this attribute is given, the attribute takes a default value of `None` (that is, no additional styling is provided).

You can use the `style` attribute on `module` and `modules`-type `jdoc` statements, but not `components`. As a general rule, `xhtml` or no value is fine for most purposes in your Joomla! template. More information on the `style` attribute is available from Joomla!'s documentation at `http://docs.joomla.org/What_is_module_chrome?`.

See also

▸ *Understanding the templateDetails.xml file*

▸ *Understanding Joomla! template positions*

▸ *Styling Joomla! error messages*

Understanding the templateDetails.xml file

The `templateDetails.xml` is vital for your Joomla! template to function correctly. It defines the metadata of your template. There are three fundamental things that this file tells Joomla!:

▸ Information about the author of the template (that's you!)

▸ The files that are used within the template

▸ The positions that Joomla! uses to position content within the template

The `templateDetails.xml` file can also provide information about a theme's color variations and other parameters.

Getting ready

If your template does not already have one, create a `templateDetails.xml` file in your template's directory. For example, if your template was called `ch2-test`, this would be in the `templates\ch2-test` directory.

How to do it...

Before we begin, we need to define a few things in our file:

```
<?xml version="1.0" encoding="utf-8"?>
<!DOCTYPE install PUBLIC "-//Joomla! 1.5//DTD template 1.0//EN"
"http://www.joomla.org/xml/dtd/1.5/template-install.dtd">
<install version="1.5" type="template">
```

The first and second lines define the version of the XML that we're using for the file, and the character encoding the file needs (stuff that needn't concern us!). The third line tells Joomla! which `version` of it our template is compatible with (1.5 in this instance), and what it is (a `template`).

Author information

The first thing that is defined within the `templateDetails.xml` file is information about the author of the template:

```
<name>ch2-test</name>
<creationDate>January 2010</creationDate>
<author>Richard Carter</author>
<authorEmail>richard@peacockcarter.co.uk</authorEmail>
<authorUrl>http://www.earlgreyandbattenburg.co.uk</authorUrl>
<version>1.0.2</version>
<description>A test of the templateDetails.xml file for Chapter 2 of
Joomla! 1.5 Templates Design Cookbook</description>
```

It allows you to define the name of the template (`ch2-test`), its creation date (`January 2010`) and the name of the author(s) of the template (`Richard Carter`), as well as their e-mail address, and website. After that, it defines the version of the template (`1.0.2`), and gives a brief description of the template, which appears when you view details of the template in the Joomla! administration panel, under **Extensions | Template Manager**:

Positions

Positions within Joomla! templates let you customize where you can place content in your template. These are defined within the template's `templateDetails.xml` file, within the `positions` element:

```
<positions>
  <position>breadcrumb</position>
  <position>left</position>
  <position>right</position>
  <position>top</position>
  <position>user1</position>
  <position>user2</position>
  <position>user3</position>
  <position>user4</position>
  <position>footer</position>
</positions>
```

As you can see, this template defines a number of positions for content to be placed within the template. You can see where these blocks appear in your Joomla! template by adding `?tp=1` to the end of your Joomla!-powered page's URL (see *Understanding Joomla! template positions*):

From the previous screenshot, you can see, among others, the **breadcrumb** block towards the top-left of the screen.

Parameters

The next thing that `templateDetails.xml` defines is a template's parameters. As we've seen, a Joomla! template can use parameters to allow variations of its color scheme, width, and other attributes.

```xml
<params>

  <param name="colorVariation" type="list" default="white"
    label="Color Variation" description="Color variation to use">
    <option value="blue">Blue</option>
    <option value="pink">Pink</option>
    <option value="red">Red</option>
    <option value="green">Green</option>
    <option value="orange">Orange</option>
    <option value="black">Black</option>
    <option value="white">White</option>
  </param>

  <param name="anotherOption" type="list" default="option1"
     label="Another Option"
     description="Another parameter option for your template">
    <option value="option1">Option 1</option>
    <option value="option2">Option 2</option>
  </param>

</params>
```

Each `<param>` element that is defined needs to have `name`, `type`, and `label` attributes defined.

The `name` attribute uniquely identifies the parameter within the template. You should not have more than one parameter in a template with the same name.

The `type` attribute tells Joomla! what type of option to create. In most cases, in Joomla! template design, you will want this value to be `list`, although there are over 20 options available for this value. Other parameter types can be found in Joomla!'s documentation at `http://docs.joomla.org/Standard_parameter_types`.

The `label` attribute is the descriptive text that appears next to the option in your Joomla! admin panel, in this case, **Color Variation** and **Another Option**:

Parameters
The parameter file /templates/ch2-test/params.ini is writable!

Color Variation White ▼

Another Option Option 1 ▼

The `description` attribute is not mandatory, so you can leave this field out if you want to. Though to help anyone using your template, it's recommended that you provide a brief overview of what the parameter does here. Similarly, the `default` value is recommended, but not required.

Parameters are optional in your template, so you don't need to have any parameters defined within your template's `templateDetails.xml` file.

Closing the XML file

Finally, we need to close the XML file:

```
</install>
```

That's it; our template's `templateDetails.xml` file is complete for now. In all, it should look similar to the following:

```xml
<?xml version="1.0" encoding="utf-8"?>
<!DOCTYPE install PUBLIC "-//Joomla! 1.5//DTD template 1.0//EN"
"http://www.joomla.org/xml/dtd/1.5/template-install.dtd">
<install version="1.5" type="template">

  <name>ch2-test</name>
  <creationDate>10/12/09</creationDate>
  <author>Richard Carter</author>
  <authorEmail>richard@peacockcarter.co.uk</authorEmail>
  <authorUrl>http://www.earlgreyandbattenburg.co.uk</authorUrl>
  <version>1.0.2</version>
  <description>A test of the templateDetails.xml file for Chapter 2
               of Joomla! 1.5 Templates Design Cookbook
  </description>
  <files>
    <filename>index.php</filename>
    <filename>templateDetails.xml</filename>
    <filename>template_thumbnail.png</filename>
  </files>
  <positions>
    <position>breadcrumb</position>
    <position>left</position>
    <position>right</position>
    <position>top</position>
  </positions>

</install>
```

How it works...

Joomla! relies on the `templateDetails.xml` file to provide it with information about the template.

There's more...

You can include a thumbnail preview of your template by adding an image called `template_thumbnail.png` into your template's directory. Make sure you add a reference to it in your `templateDetails.xml` file within the `<files>` element so that Joomla! knows it's there when the template is being installed!

```
<files>
  <!-- other files defined -->
  <filename>template_thumbnail.png</filename>
</files>
```

When you now go into your Joomla! website's admin panel, you'll see this screenshot if you hover over the name of your template in **Extensions | Template Manager**:

See also

▶ *Changing your template's color variation*

▶ *Adding a color variation*

▶ *Understanding Joomla! template positions*

Styling for component.php

You may have noticed the `component.php` file in your Joomla! template. This file contains the output of only a Joomla! component without the module output. The file is also used in place of the `index.php` file by Joomla! for special pages, such as the contact form pop-up, which is accessible by clicking on the envelope icon in your content (if enabled):

When this is clicked, Joomla! launches a pop-up window containing a contact form:

Open the `component.php` file in the *rhuk_milkyway* template (in the `templates\rhuk_milkyway` directory).

How to do it...

If you look within the `component.php` file you'll see that the `<body>` element has a class identifying it as `contentpane`:

```
<body class="contentpane">
  <jdoc:include type="message" />
  <jdoc:include type="component" />
</body>
```

This can help us distinguish pages created with `component.php` in the CSS. By adding the following CSS to the theme's `template.css` file in the `css` subdirectory, we can make changes that affect only these special pages in Joomla!:

```
body.contentpane {background: #D400AA;color: #FFF}
  .contentpane a {color: #FFF}
```

If we upload the `template.css` file and refresh the page, and trigger Joomla! to create a pop-up window again by clicking on the envelope icon, we can see the effect our CSS has on the styling of the pop-up window:

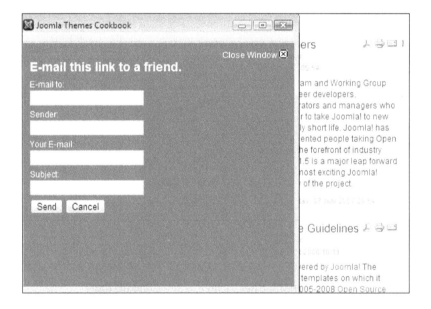

With the **Color Variation** of the Joomla! template set to **blue**, you'll see that the body color for normal Joomla! pages remains of the same color—blue. As you can see, the background color is blue, as is the pane that wraps the **Main Menu** block:

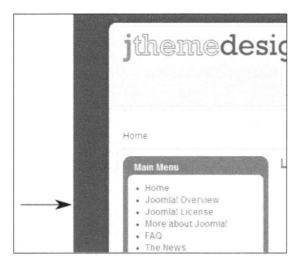

How it works...

As with normal Joomla! pages, the forms or content that form the primary content for the pop-up page are inserted with the component j doc statement:

```
<body class="contentpane">
  <jdoc:include type="message" />
  <jdoc:include type="component" />
</body>
```

The only other j doc statement is for messages, in case there are any problems with the component (for example, if the contact form is submitted with invalid information for one of its fields).

See also

▶ *Understanding Joomla! template positions*

▶ *Understanding jdoc statements*

Adding a custom favicon to your template

A **favicon** is the icon you see next to a website's address in your browser's address bar; it's an often-overlooked part of a template design and can really help your website to stand out from others. By default, your website's favicon will often be the Joomla! logo:

Getting ready...

We need to create our template's `favicon.ico` file first; it's best to create a file of 16 by 16 pixels in dimension for use as your website's favicon. For our template, we'll use a **j** from our logo's design (enlarged to the right for clarity):

 Converting your image to a .ico file

There are a number of online services which allow you to create `.ico` from more common image formats such as PNG, GIF, and JPEG, including **Dynamic Drive** (`http://tools.dynamicdrive.com/favicon/`).

How to do it...

1. Once you have settled upon a design for your template's favicon, upload it into your template's directory (`templates\rhuk_milkyway\` in this example), overwriting the existing `favicon.ico` file if necessary.

2. Once you refresh your browser, your new favicon will appear in the address bar.

 Favicon not appearing?

Sometimes you will need to entirely empty your browser's cache to see the new favicon appear.

How it works...

By adding a `favicon.ico` file in your template's directory, Joomla! adds the relevant `<link>` elements into the `<head>` element of your Joomla! template. Your website's favicon will usually appear next to the title of your website when visitors bookmark it in their browser, as well as in some browsers' tabs, including Opera (shown in the next screenshot) and Firefox. They can also add a sense of professionalism to your website for many visitors, as they provide an additional layer of "polish" to finish your Joomla! template.

There's more...

You can also specify other image formats as your `favicon.ico` file; in particular, Firefox supports animated GIF favicons.

If your favicon does not display...

You may notice that your new `favicon.ico` file does not display in place of the old version, especially in some versions of Internet Explorer. You can remedy this by clearing your browser's cache, or in some cases, by clicking on the favicon and attempting to drag it.

See also

- ▸ *Styling Joomla! error messages*
- ▸ *Understanding jdoc statements*
- ▸ *Styling for component.php*

Styling Joomla! error messages

One often-overlooked factor in designing Joomla! templates is styling Joomla!'s error messages to complement your theme. By default, these are styled by CSS in the `system.css` file found in the `templates\system\css` directory.

Getting ready

The easiest way to get Joomla! to display an error message is to attempt to log into your website with an incorrect username and password:

This inserts HTML into the page similar to the following code:

```
<dl id="system-message">
<dt class="error">Error</dt>
  <dd class="error message fade">
    <ul>
      <li>Username and password do not match or you do not have an
          account yet.
      </li>
    </ul>
  </dd>
</dl>
```

Joomla!'s `system.css` file, located in the `templates\system\css` directory dictates style for three main message styles:

- ▶ *Error*, for error messages
- ▶ *Notice*, for certain occasions that are not covered by the error style
- ▶ *Default*, which is used for other occasions not defined by the first two styles

How to do it...

We'll overwrite Joomla!'s default styling for error messages in our template's `template.css` file. Although you can change the style in the `\templates\system\css` directory, this makes upgrading your Joomla! installation more difficult, as future versions of Joomla! being installed may overwrite your changes. In our own template's `template.css` file, we ensure that the message box will be styled as we want it to be:

```
dl#system-message {
  clear: both;
  display: block;
```

```
    padding: 10px
  }

  dl#system-message ul {
    background-color: #FFF
  }
```

Next, we'll define the specific message styles:

```
  dl#system-message dd.message ul {
    color: #9C0; /* Green */
  }

  dl#system-message dd.notice ul {
    color: #fb930; /* Orange */
  }

  dl#system-message dd.message ul {
    color: #CA000; /* Red */
  }
```

Joomla!'s `system.css` file applies `display: none` to the `<dt>` (definition-list title) elements, so if we wanted these to display we would need to explicitly state:

```
  dl.system-message dt {display: block !important}
```

Take care with system-wide CSS files

We don't edit Joomla!'s own `system.css` file, as this could overwrite the style applied to system messages when another template is enabled, effectively overwriting style for other templates, which is something we should avoid!

If you now generate an error on your website, you'll see that the system message styles have changed:

Username and password do not match or you do not have an account yet.

By default, this error message would have looked like this:

How it works...

Rather than rewriting the default error message's style, we redefine the style we want for our error messages in our template's `template.css` file, meaning that other templates that rely on the system styling for error messages will still display correctly.

The error message appears in your Joomla! template where this `jdoc` statement occurs:

```
<jdoc:include type="message" />
```

See also

- ► *Understanding jdoc statements*
- ► *Understanding Joomla! template positions*

Styling Joomla! error pages

Joomla! allows for custom error pages to be displayed; you can entirely customize the look and feel of error messages to better target your website's audience.

Getting ready...

Copy the `error.php` file located in the `templates\system\` directory into your template's directory. Here we'll copy it into the `templates\rhuk_milkyway\` directory.

How to do it...

1. Firstly, you need to change your Joomla! website's settings to allow you to use a custom error page. Log in to your Joomla! administration panel (for example, at `http://example.com/administrator`), and go to **Site | Global Configuration**:

2. From here, look at the right-hand side of the screen and you'll see the **SEO Settings** panel. Set the **Use Apache mod_rewrite** setting to **Yes**, and then save the settings:

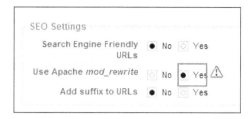

 If you're working with a default installation of Joomla!, you will also need to rename the `htaccess.txt` file in the root of your Joomla! installation to `.htaccess` (note the period character before the word `htaccess`).

3. You can then fit the error message into a more suitable template:

```php
<?php defined( '_JEXEC' ) or die( 'Restricted access' );?>
<!DOCTYPE html PUBLIC "-//W3C//DTD XHTML 1.0 Transitional//EN"
  "http://www.w3.org/TR/xhtml1/DTD/xhtml1-transitional.dtd">
<html xmlns="http://www.w3.org/1999/xhtml"
  xml:lang="<?php echo $this->language; ?>"
  lang="<?php echo $this->language; ?>" >
<head>
  <jdoc:include type="head" />
  <link rel="stylesheet" href="<?php echo $this->baseurl ?>/
templates/rhuk_milkyway/css/error.css" type="text/css" />
</head>
<body>
  <div id="error">
<h1>
<?php echo $this->error->code ?> -
<?php echo $this->error->message ?></h1>
<p><strong>
<?php echo JText::_('You may not be able to visit this page
  because of:'); ?>
</strong></p>
<ol>
<li>
 <?php echo JText::_('An out-of-date bookmark/favourite'); ?></li>
<li>
 <?php echo JText::_('A search engine that has an out-of-date
   listing for this site'); ?></li>
<li><?php echo JText::_('A mis-typed address'); ?></li>
<li>
```

```
<?php echo JText::_('You have no access to this page'); ?></li>
<li>
 <?php echo JText::_('The requested resource was not found'); ?>
</li>
<li>
<?php echo JText::_('An error has occurred while processing your
    request.'); ?>
</li>
</ol>
<p><strong>
<?php echo JText::_('Please try one of the following pages:'); ?>
</strong></p>
<ul>
<li>
 <a href="<?php echo $this->baseurl; ?> "
    title="<?php echo JText::_('Go to the home page'); ?>">
<?php echo JText::_('Home Page'); ?></a></li>
</ul>
</div>
</body>
</html>
```

4. You now need to create the `error.css` file in the `templates\rhuk_milkyway\css\` directory:

```css
/* Import primary template CSS file */
@import url("template.css");

body {
  background: #EEE;
}
#error {
  border: 1px #666 solid;
  background: #FFF;
  border-radius: 10px;
  color: #000;
  margin: 100px auto /* horiz. centre design */;
  padding: 20px;
  width: 500px;
}
#error h1 {
    color: #C00
}
#error p, #error ul {
    margin: 0 0 20px 0
}
```

5. Save your changes and upload the relevant files (`error.php` and `error.css`) into the relevant directories (`templates\rhuk_milkyway\` and `templates\rhuk_milkyway\css` respectively). If you now attempt to load a page that does not exist on your Joomla! website, you can see the new error page style appear:

How it works...

When Joomla! encounters an error, it looks for the `error.php` file in the current template's directory, and if it fails to do so, it looks for the `error.php` file in the `templates\system` directory.

 As the `error.php` file is separate from Joomla! and its framework, you cannot make use of modules or `jdoc` statements in the error template.

There's more...

One issue with Joomla! is that error pages return a **200 OK** response code when they display an error page, which can cause problems with search engines, as pages that do not technically exist on your website can be found in search engine results pages. Typically, a **404 not found** response is expected if the page does not exist, for which we can modify Joomla!'s behavior. Simply open your template's `index.php` file, and insert the following PHP code above your template's `<!DOCTYPE>` declaration:

```
<?php
defined( '_JEXEC' ) or die( 'Restricted access' );?>

<?php
if ($this->error->code == '404') {
```

```
  header("HTTP/1.0 404 Not Found");
} ?>

<!DOCTYPE html PUBLIC "-//W3C//DTD XHTML 1.0 Transitional//EN"
  "http://www.w3.org/TR/xhtml1/DTD/xhtml1-transitional.dtd">

<!-- remainder of your Joomla! template -->
```

If you now save and upload this file (if necessary), your Joomla! website will return a **404** response rather than a **200** response, making your website much more search engine friendly.

See also

> ▸ *Styling for component.php*

3
Theming the Details

This chapter looks at customizing your Joomla! template further, including:

- ▸ Styling the search module
- ▸ Styling the search component
- ▸ Using template overrides in your Joomla! template
- ▸ Customizing the breadcrumb
- ▸ Styling pagination
- ▸ Linking back to the top of your page
- ▸ Adding a random background image to your Joomla! template

Introduction

Although we've seen how to alter much of our Joomla! website, there's still much we can do to improve and polish our Joomla! template to perfection.

Styling the search module

Joomla! is a powerful content management system that is capable of supporting websites with hundreds and even thousands of pages. When websites become this large, it's often important to provide your website's visitors with a search feature as a means of locating the information on your website that they are looking for. One option that Joomla! provides for your visitors to search your website is the **search module**, which is a block displayed within your template.

Getting ready

Identify the `class` or `id` assigned to your Joomla! template's search form, which is assigned by a `jdoc include` statement within your template's `index.php` file. In the *rhuk_milkyway* template—the one that we've been working with—the search feature is assigned to the `user4` block by default with this `jdoc` statement:

```
<jdoc:include type="modules" name="user4" />
```

It appears to the top-right of the template:

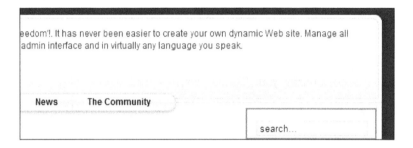

If we now look at the page's HTML source, the HTML generated by Joomla! for the search feature looks like this:

```
<div id="search">
 <form action="index.php" method="post">
  <div class="search">
    <input name="searchword" id="mod_search_searchword"
          maxlength="20" alt="Search" class="inputbox"
          type="text" size="20" value="search."
          onblur="if(this.value=='')this.value='search...';"
          onfocus="if(this.value=='search...') this.value='';" />
  </div>
    <input type="hidden" name="task"    value="search" />
    <input type="hidden" name="option" value="com_search" />
    <input type="hidden" name="Itemid" value=1 />
 </form>
```

This means that we can apply CSS to `#search` to style our template's search box.

How to do it...

1. Open your template's primary stylesheet file, which is usually called `template.css`, and is located in the `templates\rhuk_milkyway\css\` directory of your Joomla! installation. The *rhuk_milkyway* template already defines the style for the form as follows:

```
#search {
    float: right;
    width:320px;
    margin-top: -20px;
    margin-right: 30px;
    height: 40px;
    overflow: hidden;
    text-align:right;
}
```

2. By adding CSS to change the search field's state when a visitor focuses within it, you can help improve your Joomla! template by orientating visitors to their whereabouts on the page:

```
#search input[type='text']:focus {
border-color: #09C /* blue */

}
```

3. Once you've uploaded the altered `template.css` file, you will now see a blue border surrounding the search field:

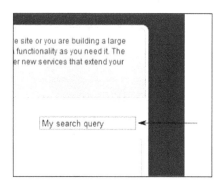

How it works...

By using the **CSS pseudo-class** :focus, the browser changes the attributes we define to make it clearer to our website's visitors that their input device (for example, keyboard) is focused on the search input field.

> Internet Explorer versions 7 and below do not support the :focus pseudo-class. You can provide support in Internet Explorer for this feature of CSS with the use of JavaScript; see http://james.padolsey. com/javascript/fixing-focus-in-internet-explorer/.

See also

> ▸ *Understanding Joomla! template positions*
>
> ▸ *Styling the search component*

Styling the search component

Along with providing the search module, which is embedded within your Joomla! template depending on the module position it is assigned to, there is the Joomla! search component.

Getting ready

Firstly, you need to access the search component on your Joomla! website. You can do this by visiting `http://example.com/index.php?option=com_search`, assuming that your Joomla! installation is installed in the root directory of the `example.com` domain. With the *rhuk_milkyway* template as your currently enabled template, you should see that the search component looks like this:

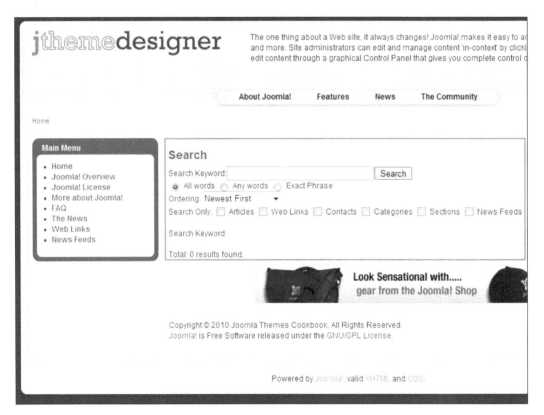

Open your template's primary CSS file; for our example, this is `templates\rhuk_milkyway\css\template.css`. It is also worth studying the source of the search component page; you'll find that the search form is contained within a `<form>` element identified with an `id` of `searchForm`.

How to do it...

1. In your template's CSS file (`template.css`), begin by styling the overall form first:

   ```
   form#searchForm {
   background: #E5F1FD;
   border: 1px #0C3A6D solid;
   border-radius: 10px;
   padding: 10px
   }
   ```

    Some browsers do not yet support the `border-radius` property in CSS, so you may just see the search form with squared corners.

   This changes the look of the search form as follows:

2. Next, you'll style the search query field, which is identifiable by the `#search_searchword` id:

   ```
   #searchForm #search_searchword {
   border: 2px #0C3A6D solid;
   color: #0C3A6D
   }
   ```

This helps to distinguish the search field from the other fields in the form:

3. Lastly, you'll add some padding to the table cells used to lay out the search component form to provide a little more space between inputs to prevent visitors accidentally clicking:

```
#searchForm table td {
padding: 5px
}
```

That's the search form styled!

How it works...

By applying CSS to the relevant elements generated by Joomla!, it's possible to redefine what the search form provided by Joomla!'s search component looks like.

See also

▶ *Styling the search module*

▶ *Using template overrides in your Joomla! template*

Using template overrides in your Joomla! template

You can use template overrides in your Joomla! template to redefine the output HTML that Joomla! creates for the modules and components on your installation. This can be useful when you are unable to achieve the style you want for your Joomla! template with the markup provided in the base template that you are using.

Getting ready

In this example, you'll be changing the search component's **Search** button, as displayed at `http://example.com/index.php?option=com_search`, assuming that you have Joomla! installed at `example.com`:

Search
Search Keyword: [   ] [Search]
⦿ All words ○ Any words ○ Exact Phrase
Ordering: Newest First ▾
Search Only: ☐ Articles ☐ Web Links ☐ Contacts ☐ Categories ☐ Sections ☐ News Feeds
Search Keyword
Total: 0 results found.

One such thing that you may want to change is the **Search** button. In this example, we'll change it to a `<input type= "image" />` so that we're able to use an image for the **Search** button rather than the browser's default rendering of the `<button>` element that we can see in the previous screenshot.

How to do it...

1. Save the search button graphic that you want to use in place of the **Search** button in the `templates\rhuk_milkyway\images` directory as `search.png`:

2. Next, you need to copy the contents of the `default_form.php` file located in the `components\com_search\views\search\tmpl` directory of your Joomla! installation into the `templates\rhuk_milkyway\html\com_search\views\search` directory. You may need to create the `com_search` subdirectory and its child directories (`view` and `search`) if they do not already exist. Locate the line that reads:

```
<button name="Search" onclick="this.form.submit()"
        class="button"><?php echo JText::_( 'Search' );?>
</button>
```

3. Replace this line with:

```
<input type="image" name="Search" onclick="this.form.submit()"
    src="<?php echo $this->baseurl ?>templates/rhuk_milkyway/images/
        search.png"
    alt="<?php echo JText::_( 'Search' );?>" />
```

4. Your new search component form now looks like this:

How it works...

By default, Joomla! looks in a component's own directory within the currently enabled Joomla! template for a custom template override. If Joomla! fails to find this file, it looks in the `\components` directory for the relevant file with which to generate the required HTML by the component.

See also

▶ *Styling the search module*

▶ *Styling the search component*

Customizing the breadcrumb

The larger your website gets, the more important it is to make use of Joomla!'s breadcrumb feature.

Getting ready

To start redefining your breadcrumb's style, open the `template.css` file for your template; use the *rhuk_milkyway* template for this demonstration. This means that your CSS file will be located in the `templates\rhuk_milkyway\css` directory of your Joomla! installation. If you visit a page other than the home page in your Joomla! website, you'll be able to see the breadcrumb.

As you can see, the *rhuk_milkyway* template defines the style for the breadcrumb in the `template.css` file.

```
span.pathway {
  display: block;
  margin: 0 20px;
  height: 16px;
  line-height: 16px;
  overflow: hidden;
}
```

The HTML that defines the breadcrumb for the **Features** page is as shown:

```
<div id="pathway">
 <span class="breadcrumbs pathway">
  <a href="http://example.com/" class="pathway">Home</a>
  <img src=" /templates/rhuk_milkyway/images/arrow.png" alt="" />
   Features
 </span>
</div>
```

How to do it...

1. You can customize the breadcrumb by changing the CSS, and altering the color and size of the breadcrumb's content:

```
span.pathway {
  color: #666;
  font-size: 90%;
  display: block;
  margin: 0 20px;
  height: 16px;
  line-height: 16px;
  overflow: hidden;
}
```

2. Once the altered CSS file has been uploaded, you can see your changes:

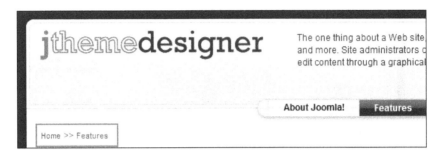

3. The next step to customizing your breadcrumb is to alter the image used for the separator arrows, located at \templates\rhuk_milkyway\images\arrow.png. You'll replace this image with your own new one (which has been enlarged in this image to make it easier to view).

4. Once uploaded, your new breadcrumb looks a little more fitting for your website:

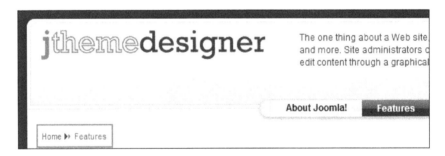

How it works...

By targeting specific ids and classes with CSS and changing an image in the images directory of our template, we can subtly change our template to distinguish it from others without a great deal of work.

See also

▶ *Styling the search module*

▶ *Styling pagination*

Styling pagination

Some content in your Joomla! website may run over multiple pages (for example, some search results). By styling pagination, you can again help to distinguish your Joomla! template from others.

Getting ready

Open your template's primary stylesheet; generally, this will be called `template.css`, and is located in the `templates\rhuk_milkyway\css\` directory if we are using the *rhuk_milkyway* template (as we are for this demonstration).

It is also worth bearing in mind the typical structure of the pagination feature within the HTML. We can find this by searching for a common word such as "the" or "Joomla!" on our website.

```
<span class="pagination">

  <span>&laquo;</span>
  <span>Start</span>
  <span>Prev</span><strong>
  <span>1</span></strong>

  <strong>
   <a href=" index.php?searchword=Joomla&amp;searchphrase=all&amp;
    Itemid=1&amp; option=com_search&amp;limitstart=20" title="2">2</a>
  </strong>

  <strong>
   <a href=" index.php?searchword=Joomla&amp;searchphrase=all&amp;
   Itemid=1&amp; option=com_search&amp;limitstart=40" title="3">3
   </a></strong>

   <a href=" index.php?searchword=Joomla&amp;searchphrase=all&amp;
    Itemid=1&amp; option=com_search&amp;limitstart=20" title="Next">
    Next </a>

   <a href=" index.php?searchword=Joomla&amp;searchphrase=all&amp;
    Itemid=1&amp; option=com_search&amp;limitstart=40"
    title="End">End</a>

  <span>&raquo;</span>

</span>
```

Our primary interest in the previous part is the `.pagination` class assigned to the `<span>` element that contains the pagination feature's content. By default, the pagination (as seen on the search results page) looks like this:

« Start Prev **1** 2 3 Next End »

How to do it...

1. Now that you are aware of the relevant class to style, you can add it to your template's stylesheet, with the aim of making the pagination less obtrusive with the surrounding content of your pages:

```
.pagination {
color: #666;
font-size: 90%
}

.pagination a {
color: #F07 !important /* pink */
}
```

2. Once you've uploaded the newer stylesheet, you'll be able to see the new pagination style, which will appear smaller than before, and with pink-colored links.

« Start Prev **1** 2 3 Next End »

Producing more semantic markup for pagination

As you can see in the previous section, the HTML that Joomla! currently generates for the pagination feature is quite verbose—unnecessarily long and untidy. We'll change our template's `pagination.php` file to use more semantic (meaningful) HTML for this feature by adding each item to a list item within an unordered list element (`<ul>`).

The HTML for pagination is defined within the `pagination.php` file, located in the `html` directory of your template. If you edit this file, remember that you need to escape certain characters such as double quotation marks, that is, `<div class="list-footer">` should read `<div class=\"list-footer\">`. You can mitigate the need to do this by using single quotation marks (`'`) rather than double quotation marks (`"`).

Other templates using semantic markup

The **Beez template** that comes with the default Joomla! installation already provides semantically correct markup for pagination.

1. Open the `pagination.php` file and you will see four PHP functions (assuming that you are looking within the _rhuk_milkyway_ template), but the function which is of interest to us is the `pagination_list_render` PHP function. Currently, the code for this function looks like this:

```php
function pagination_list_render($list)
{
    // Initialize variables
    $html = "<span class=\"pagination\">";
    $html .= '<span>&laquo;</span>'.$list['start']['data'];
    $html .= $list['previous']['data'];

    foreach( $list['pages'] as $page )
    {
        if($page['data']['active']) {
            $html .= '<strong>';
        }

        $html .= $page['data'];

        if($page['data']['active']) {
            $html .= '</strong>';
        }
    }

    $html .= $list['next']['data'];
    $html .= $list['end']['data'];
    $html .= '<span>&raquo;</span>';

    $html .= "</span>";
    return $html;
}
```

2. You can see that Joomla! builds up the HTML to insert into the page by using the `$html` PHP variable. All you need to change is the HTML you can see:

```php
function pagination_list_render($list)
{
    // Initialize variables
    $html = "<ul class=\"pagination\">";
    $html .= '<li class="page-previous">&laquo;</li>' . '<li>' .
             $list['start']['data'] . '</li>';
    $html .= '<li>' . $list['previous']['data'] . '</li>';

    foreach( $list['pages'] as $page )
    {
```

```
        if ($page ['data'] ['active']) {
            $html .= '<li>';
        }

        $html .= '<strong class="active">' . $page ['data'] .
                    '</strong>';

        if ($page ['data'] ['active']) {
            $html .= '</li>';
        }
    }

    $html .= '<li>' . $list ['next'] ['data'] . '</li>';
    $html .= '<li>' .   $list ['end'] ['data'] . '</li>';
    $html .= '<li class="page-next">&raquo;</li>';

    $html .= "</ul>";
    return $html;
}
```

3. If you now upload the `pagination.php` file and refresh the page, you'll see that the previous style that you had defined only partially styles the newer HTML:

4. If you add the following CSS to your template's `template.css` file, everything will be styled as you intended before:

```
ul.pagination {
    list-style-type: none
}

ul.pagination li {
    display: inline
}
```

5. Once uploaded, your new pagination is complete:

« Start Prev **1** 2 3 Next End »

How it works...

By applying CSS to the relevant `ids` and `classes` specified in the HTML for Joomla!'s pagination feature, it's possible to quite drastically alter the pagination's appearance for your Joomla! template. It's also possible to change the HTML generated by Joomla! in some circumstances, as we saw with our template's `pagination.php` file. One benefit of changing the HTML that Joomla! outputs is that you can add `classes` and `ids` that make it easier to style elements of your Joomla! website with CSS.

See also

▸ _Customizing the breadcrumb_

Linking back to the top of your page

If your website contains a number of very long articles or pieces of content, it's wise to include a **back to the top** link at the bottom of each page.

Getting ready

Open your Joomla! template's `index.php` file. For the purposes of this example, we'll be using the _rhuk_milkyway_ template, though the technique can be applied to any Joomla! template.

How to do it...

1. Search for the following snippet of code in your template:

```
<table class="nopad">
<tr valign="top">
  <td>
    <jdoc:include type="component" />
    <jdoc:include type="modules" name="footer" style="xhtml"/>
  </td>
```

2. Create an anchor called `top` above the line where the statement
   `<jdoc:include type="component" />` is included in your page:

```
<table class="nopad">
<tr valign="top">
  <td>
    <a name="top"> </a>
    <jdoc:include type="component" />
    <jdoc:include type="modules" name="footer" style="xhtml"/>
  </td>
```

3. Beneath the `include` statement that includes the content, now add the link to the
   top of the page:

```
<table class="nopad">
<tr valign="top">
  <td>
    <a name="top"> </a>
    <jdoc:include type="component" />
    <p class="top-of-page">
      <a href="#top" title="Top of this page">Top of this page</a>
    </p>
    <jdoc:include type="modules" name="footer" style="xhtml"/>
  </td>
```

4. You can now add a little style for your link by defining CSS for `p.top-of-page` in
   your template's `template.css` file:

```
p.top-of-page {
 color: #666;
 font-size: 90%;
}

p.top-of-page a {
 color: #09C /* blue */
}
```

5. Once the changed files have been uploaded, you can see your link appear towards the bottom of every page in your Joomla! website:

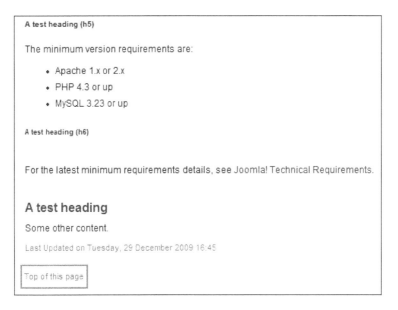

How it works...

The `<jdoc:include type="component" />` statement inserts the page's content into our Joomla! template, so this is where we want to allow our website's visitors to skip back to the top. Giving the value `#top` for the `href` attribute in the `link` element (inserted below the content) creates a link to an anchor called `top` within the page, which we create above the content block in the form `<a name="top"> </a>`.

There's more...

There is an extension available for Joomla! that provides similar functionality; it's called **Return to Top for Content Items,** and is available from the Joomla! website at `http://extensions.joomla.org/extensions/structure-a-navigation/site-navigation/5617`.

 Downloading the extension requires you to be logged into the extension developer's website.

Rather than inserting a **Return to top** link in every page on your website, it allows you to insert these links wherever you need to within your content by inserting `{rt}` into your page's content.

However, adding the link to your template is better for your website's performance, as every module or plugin that your Joomla! website has enabled will slow down the loading time of the website for your visitors.

See also

 ▸ *Styling the search module*
 ▸ *Styling pagination*

Adding a random background image to your Joomla! template

In distinguishing your Joomla! template from others, there are a number of extensions for Joomla! to help you, including one that allows you to display a random image as your template's background image for the `<body>` element.

Getting ready

You need to install the extension called **Random Background**. You can find the file's download link on the Joomla! website at `http://extensions.joomla.org/extensions/style-a-design/templating/6054`. Once you have saved the extension files somewhere on your computer, log in to your website's Joomla! administration panel (if Joomla! is installed at `example.com`, the administration panel is typically accessible at `example.com/administrator`), and select the **Install/Uninstall** option from the **Extensions** option in the primary navigation:

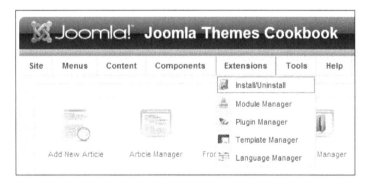

You will then be presented with a form, from where you can upload the extension's `.zip` file. Select the file from your computer, and then click on the **Upload File & Install** button:

Once complete, you should receive a confirmation message:

Setting relevant permissions for installing the module

If you have problems installing the module, you may receive an error message like the following one:

The error is most likely because two directories on your server do not have sufficient permissions:

- \tmp
- \modules

Use Joomla!'s FTP layer to manage the necessary file permissions for you. You can edit Joomla!'s configuration file, which is called `configuration.php`, in the root of your Joomla! website. Simply add these variables into the file if they don't exist already:

```
var $ftp_host = ''; // your FTP host, e.g. ftp.example.com or just
example.com, depending on your host
var $ftp_port = '';  // usually 21
var $ftp_user = ''; // your FTP username
var $ftp_pass = ''; // your FTP password
var $ftp_root = ''; // usually / or the directory of your Joomla!
install
var $ftp_enable = '1';  // 1 = enabled
```

How to do it...

1. Firstly, you need to enable the extension from Joomla!'s **Module Manager** in the administration panel:

2. From the list of available extensions on your website, you'll need to check the box next to the **Background** extension:

3. Now click on the **Background** link to view the extension's settings. Notice that the extension needs to be assigned to a position within your template to function.

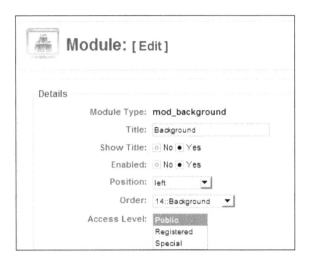

4. Towards the right of the screen, there are options for the extension. Of particular interest to us is the value of the **Choose random image** option that we need to change to **Yes**.

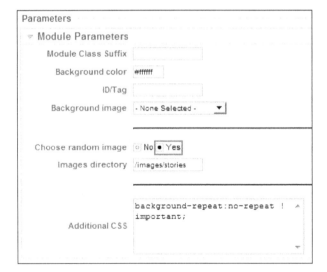

5. Once the extension has been installed and enabled, you can upload the images you want to appear as background images on your Joomla! website by using Joomla!'s **Media Manager** feature. You can also customize the CSS in the **Additional CSS** field to allow the background image to repeat either vertically (`background-repeat: repeat-y`) or horizontally (`background-repeat: repeat-x`). When you refresh the frontend of your Joomla! website (that is, not the administration panel), you'll see a random image appear at the top-left of the template.

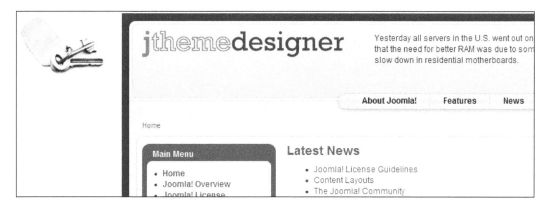

See also

▸ *Styling the search module*

▸ *Styling pagination*

4

Custom Page Templates

This chapter deals with creating individual custom page templates for your Joomla! template, and includes:

- ► Understanding Module Chrome in Joomla!
- ► Customizing the error page in Joomla!
- ► Creating a custom site offline page

Introduction

Depending on the type of website you're using Joomla! to manage, you may find that you need to make use of custom templates for your website. Custom templates can be used to further customize different aspects of your Joomla! website, from changing the **Page not found** (**404**) error page to generating revenue, through displaying advertisements on your website. Joomla! gives you the opportunity to change these aspects of your website.

Understanding Module Chrome in Joomla!

One element of Joomla! templates that is very specific to Joomla! is Module Chrome. **Module Chrome** allows you as a Joomla! template designer to have greater control over the code that surrounds each module that Joomla! outputs.

Getting ready

View your Joomla! website in your browser.

How to do it...

1. Look at the menu to the left of the template surrounded by a colored, rounded border.

2. If you view the source of the home page in the *rhuk_milkyway* template, you'll see that the corresponding XHTML for this is surrounded by "Module Chrome":

```
<div class="module_menu">
  <div>
    <div>
      <div>
        <!—rounded content-->
      </div>
    </div>
  </div>
</div>
```

3. This is the `rounded` Module Chrome. Another Module Chrome is `none`, which applies nothing around your content—xhtml wraps the module in a `div` tag with the `class` attribute referencing the name of the module:

```
<div class="moduletable_menu">
  <!-- module content -->
</div>
```

There's more...

The `outline` Module Chrome is what is applied when you append `tp=1` to the end of the page's address in your browser to display Joomla!'s template positions, which displays labels that tell you which Module Chrome is applied to which module.

user1[xhtml outline]

- Joomla! License Guidelines
- Content Layouts
- The Joomla! Community
- Welcome to Joomla!
- Newsflash 4

See also

▸ *Customizing the error page in Joomla!*

▸ *Creating a custom site offline page*

Customizing the error page in Joomla!

It's the small touches to a website that can often make the difference between a poorly designed website and a well-designed website. One such small touch is to provide a customized error page that is displayed when a visitor to your website attempts to view a page on your website that doesn't exist.

Getting ready

Copy the `error.php` file in the `templates\system` directory into your template's directory. For this example, we'll copy it into the `templates\rhuk_milkyway` directory. This technique is known as **template overriding** in Joomla!.

How to do it...

Visually, we're aiming to create something that looks a little like this:

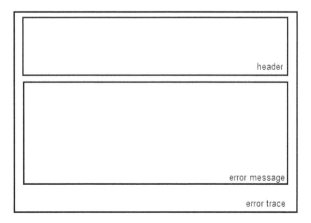

At the moment, our error page's file looks like this:

```
<!DOCTYPE html PUBLIC "-//W3C//DTD XHTML 1.0 Transitional//EN"
  "http://www.w3.org/TR/xhtml1/DTD/xhtml1-transitional.dtd">
<html xmlns="http://www.w3.org/1999/xhtml"
 xml:lang="<?php echo $this->language; ?>"
 lang="<?php echo $this->language; ?>"
 dir="<?php echo $this->direction; ?>">
<head>
 <title>
   <?php echo $this->error->code ?> - <?php echo $this->title; ?>
 </title>
 <link rel="stylesheet"
  href="<?php echo $this->baseurl; ?>/templates/system/css/error.css"
  type="text/css" />
 <?php if($this->direction == 'rtl') : ?>
 <link rel="stylesheet" href="<?php echo $this->baseurl ?>/templates/
system/css/error_rtl.css" type="text/css" />
 <?php endif; ?>
</head>
<body>
  <div align="center">
  <div id="outline">
  <div id="errorboxoutline">
  <div id="errorboxheader">
    <?php echo $this->error->code ?> -
    <?php echo $this->error->message ?>
  </div>
  <div id="errorboxbody">
   <p><strong>
    <?php echo JText::_('You may not be able to visit this page
       because of:'); ?>
   </strong></p>
   <ol>
    <li>
     <?php echo JText::_('An out-of-date bookmark/favourite'); ?>
    </li>
    <li>
     <?php echo JText::_('A search engine that has an out-of-date
       listing for this site'); ?>
    </li>
    <li><?php echo JText::_('A mis-typed address'); ?></li>
    <li>
      <?php echo JText::_('You have no access to this page'); ?>
    </li>
```

```
  <li>
    <?php echo JText::_('The requested resource was not found'); ?>
  </li>
  <li>
    <?php echo JText::_('An error has occurred while processing your
      request.'); ?>
  </li>
  </ol>
  <p><strong>
   <?php echo JText::_('Please try one of the following pages:'); ?>
  </strong></p>
  <p>
   <ul>
    <li>
      <a href="<?php echo $this->baseurl; ?>/index.php"
         title="<?php echo JText::_('Go to the home page'); ?>">
      <?php echo JText::_('Home Page'); ?></a></li>
   </ul>
  </p>
  <p>
  <?php echo JText::_('If difficulties persist, please contact
     the system administrator of this site.'); ?>
  </p>
 <div id="techinfo">
  <p><?php echo $this->error->message; ?></p>
  <p>
   <?php if($this->debug) :
    echo $this->renderBacktrace();
   endif; ?>
  </p>
 </div>
 </div>
 </div>
 </div>
 </div>
</body>
</html>
```

1. First, you need to alter the path to the stylesheet. Locate the following code:

    ```
    <link rel="stylesheet" href="<?php echo $this->baseurl; ?>/
    templates/system/css/error.css" type="text/css" />
    <?php if($this->direction == 'rtl') : ?>
       <link rel="stylesheet" href="<?php echo $this->baseurl ?>/
    templates/system/css/error_rtl.css" type="text/css" />
    <?php endif; ?>
    ```

2. Change the path to reference your template's stylesheet. Remember to include the base URL PHP snippet (`<?php echo $this->baseurl; ?>`) to ensure that your stylesheet works.

```
<link rel="stylesheet" href="<?php echo $this->baseurl; ?>/
templates/rhuk_milkyway/css/template.css" type="text/css" />
```

3. Next, make use of the *rhuk_milkyway* template's header and footer and wrap these around the content in the error template:

```
<!DOCTYPE html PUBLIC "-//W3C//DTD XHTML 1.0 Transitional//EN"
 "http://www.w3.org/TR/xhtml1/DTD/xhtml1-transitional.dtd">
<html xmlns="http://www.w3.org/1999/xhtml"
  xml:lang="<?php echo $this->language; ?>"
  lang="<?php echo $this->language; ?>"
  dir="<?php echo $this->direction; ?>">
<head>
 <title>
  <?php echo $this->error->code ?> -
  <?php echo $this->title; ?></title>
  <link rel="stylesheet" href="<?php echo $this->baseurl; ?>/
templates/rhuk_milkyway/css/template.css" type="text/css" />
  <?php if($this->direction == 'rtl') : ?>
  <link rel="stylesheet" href="<?php echo $this->baseurl ?>/
templates/system/css/error_rtl.css" type="text/css" />
  <?php endif; ?>
</head>
<body>
  <div class="center" align="center">
  <div id="wrapper">
  <div id="wrapper_r">
  <div id="header">
   <div id="header_l">
    <div id="header_r">
     <div id="logo"></div>
    </div>
   </div>
  </div>

  <div class="clr"></div>
  <div id="maincolumn_full">
   <table class="nopad">
    <tr valign="top">
      <div id="errorboxoutline">
      <div id="errorboxheader">
        <?php echo $this->error->code ?> -
```

```php
    <?php echo $this->error->message ?></div>
<div id="errorboxbody">
<p><strong>
<?php echo JText::_('You may not be able to visit this page
   because of:'); ?></strong></p>
<ol>
 <li>
<?php echo JText::_('An out-of-date bookmark/favourite'); ?>
</li>
 <li>
 <?php echo JText::_('A search engine that has an
    out-of-date listing for this site'); ?>
 </li>
 <li><?php echo JText::_('A mis-typed address'); ?></li>
 <li>
<?php echo JText::_('You have no access to this page'); ?>
 </li>
 <li><?php echo JText::_('The requested resource was not
        found'); ?></li>
 <li><?php echo JText::_('An error has occurred while
        processing your request.'); ?></li>
</ol>
<p><strong>
<?php echo JText::_('Please try one of the following
   pages:'); ?></strong></p>
<p>
 <ul>
   <li>
  <a href="<?php echo $this->baseurl; ?>/index.php"
   title="<?php echo JText::_('Go to the home page'); ?>">
  <?php echo JText::_('Home Page'); ?></a></li>
 </ul>
</p>
<p>
<?php echo JText::_('If difficulties persist, please contact
   the system administrator of this site.'); ?>
</p>
  <div id="techinfo">
  <p><?php echo $this->error->message; ?></p>
  <p>
    <?php if($this->debug) :
       echo $this->renderBacktrace();
      endif; ?>
  </p>
  </div>
</div>
```

```
              </div>
           </tr>
         </table>

              <div id="maindivider"></div>
           </div>
            <div class="clr"></div>
           </div>
            <div class="clr"></div>
           </div>

            <div id="whitebox_b">
             <div id="whitebox_bl">
              <div id="whitebox_br"></div>
             </div>
            </div>
           </div>

            <div id="footerspacer"></div>
           </div>

       </div>
       </div>
       </body>
       </html>
```

4. When an error is now encountered, visitors will see a more consistent error page:

jthemedesigner

404 - Component not found
You may not be able to visit this page because of:

1. An out-of-date bookmark/favourite
2. A search engine that has an out-of-date listing for this site
3. A mis-typed address
4. You have no access to this page
5. The requested resource was not found
6. An error has occurred while processing your request.

Please try one of the following pages:

- Home Page

If difficulties persist, please contact the system administrator of this site.

To view your error page, attempt to visit a page on your website that does not exist; for example, if your Joomla! website is installed at `http://www.example.com/`, try visiting `http://www.example.com/not-a-page`.

How it works...

When Joomla! encounters an error, it looks for the `error.php` file in your template. By customizing the contents of this file, we can customize the way the errors appear to our Joomla! website's visitors.

One restriction of the `error.php` file is that you cannot make use of modules or use `<jdoc:include>` statements in it, as the error page needs to remain as separate as possible from your template so that it can be used for other templates too.

See also

▸ *Creating a custom site offline page*

▸ *Using template overrides in your Joomla! template*

Creating a custom site offline page

Sometimes, it is necessary to temporarily disable access to your website to allow you to perform maintenance on your website. By default, Joomla!'s offline page looks like this:

Getting ready

You can customize this view by changing the logo displayed to your site's logo. To do this, you need to open the `offline.php` file in the `templates\system` directory, and copy this file to your template's directory; in this case, we'll copy it to the `templates\rhuk_milkyway` directory.

 The login form needs to remain, as this allows you to log into your website and view the changes that you're making while it is in "offline" mode.

How to do it...

1. Within the `offline.php` file, locate the following XHTML:

   ```
   <div id="frame" class="outline">
   <img src="images/joomla_logo_black.jpg"
        alt="joomla Logo" align="middle" />
   ```

2. You can change the `src` attribute of the image to the path of your website's newer logo, setting the `alt` attribute to the name of the website as stored by Joomla!:

   ```
   <div id="frame" class="outline">
   <img src="/templates/rhuk_milkyway/images/mw_joomla_logo.png"
        alt="<?php echo $mainframe->getCfg('sitename'); ?>"
        align="middle" />
   ```

3. Just below the logo, the title of your Joomla! website is inserted. Remove the following line of code as your logo contains the name of the website already:

   ```
   <h1><?php echo $mainframe->getCfg('sitename'); ?></h1>
   ```

4. Once you've uploaded the `offline.php` file, you'll see the changes once the website has been turned offline:

5. To turn your Joomla! website offline into 'maintenance mode', log in to the Joomla! administration panel, and navigate to **Site | Global Configuration**. From here, set the value of **Site Offline** to **Yes**:

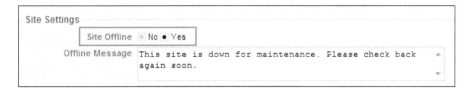

There's more...

You can edit the text that is displayed on the offline template in Joomla!'s administration panel. Log into your website's administration panel and select **Global Configuration** from the **Site** option. From here, you can set the text that appears below the logo:

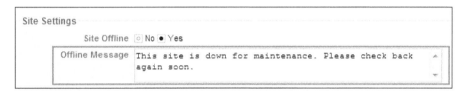

Click on **Apply** at the top-right of the screen after changing the text and you'll see that the changes appear when your website is in "offline" mode.

 Note that changes to Joomla!'s core code such as this can be overwritten by a future upgrade, so you may need to make this change again if you upgrade your version of Joomla!.

See also

▶ *Customizing the error pages in Joomla!*

5
Styling Joomla! for Print

This chapter deals with styling your Joomla! website for printing, and covers:

- How to assign a print stylesheet to your Joomla! template
- An overview of known browser display inconsistencies with print styling
- Styling images, content, and links on your document

Introduction

An often-overlooked aspect of creating custom templates and designs for content management systems such as Joomla! is styling content for print. Despite the increasing use of the Internet to distribute content, visitors still do print content from websites. In particular, if your website contains general news articles or long pieces of content on a particular topic, your website's visitors may well be printing your content, so it's worth your while taking the time to create a functioning print style for your website.

Starting your print stylesheet

Once you have linked your print stylesheet within your Joomla! template file, you can begin defining the style your visitors will see, should they attempt to print a page on your website.

Getting ready

As per our example, take the *rhuk_milkyway* template, which is installed by default within Joomla!. On screen, a typical page on your website may look like this:

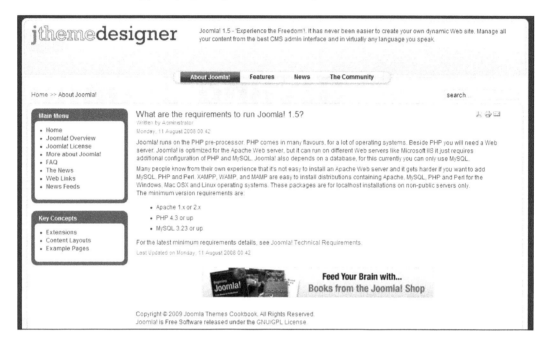

Although the previous design looks nice on the screen, it does not provide ideal styling for those visitors wanting to print our website:

- The background color and images set in the `<body>` tag would be very intensive on your ink cartridges to print, as would other areas of concentrated color.

- Quite a large portion of the screen is dedicated to navigation; this isn't necessary for print as the links won't work.

- Advertisements can lose their effectiveness in print, especially as visitors cannot click on them. Some banners (especially animated banners) do not necessarily indicate the destination of the advert.

Your Joomla! website will probably already have a `print` function available, linked to with a printer icon to the right of content in the *rhuk_milkyway* template:

When selected by a visitor to your website, a pop up of the page styled more appropriately for printing is displayed:

> **What are the requirements to run Joomla! 1.5?**
>
> Written by Administrator
>
> Monday, 11 August 2008 00:42
>
> Joomla! runs on the PHP pre-processor. PHP comes in many flavours, for a lot of operating systems. Beside PHP you will need a Web server. Joomla! is optimized for the Apache Web server, but it can run on different Web servers like Microsoft IIS it just requires additional configuration of PHP and MySQL. Joomla! also depends on a database, for this currently you can only use MySQL.
>
> Many people know from their own experience that it's not easy to install an Apache Web server and it gets harder if you want to add MySQL, PHP and Perl. XAMPP, WAMP, and MAMP are easy to install distributions containing Apache, MySQL, PHP and Perl for the Windows, Mac OSX and Linux operating systems. These packages are for localhost installations on non-public servers only.
> The minimum version requirements are:
>
> - Apache 1.x or 2.x
> - PHP 4.3 or up
> - MySQL 3.23 or up
>
> For the latest minimum requirements details, see Joomla! Technical Requirements.
>
> Last Updated on Monday, 11 August 2008 00:42

Although we can see that some of the issues mentioned here are addressed, this is not an ideal **print stylesheet**, as visitors who use their browsers to print rather than the print pop up will not necessarily see an acceptable version of the website to print.

How to do it...

1. Create a new CSS file called `print.css` in the `css` subdirectory of your Joomla! template's `template` directory; in this case, create this file in the `templates\rhuk_milkyway\css\` directory.

   Our very simple print stylesheet will ensure that the foreground color is set to black and the background color of the page is set to white.

   ```
   body {
   background: #FFF;
   color: #000
   }
   ```

How it works...

When printing or viewing a web page's print preview, most browsers will use the stylesheet indicated within the `<head>` portion of the document with the `media="print"` type. Failing that, style referenced by the `media="all"` type will be applied during print.

There's more...

If the print pop up has an odd-colored background, try altering the style applied to `#contentpane` in your template's CSS file (`template.css`).

It's useful to be able to view your print stylesheet as you add to it, without having to print and reprint your web page. An easy way to do this is with Firefox and the Web Developer toolbar, available from the Mozilla website: `https://addons.mozilla.org/en-US/firefox/addon/60`.

1. Once you have installed this add-on to Firefox, open your Joomla! website in Firefox and view a page. In the following example, we've chosen the **About Joomla!** page linked to top of the page.

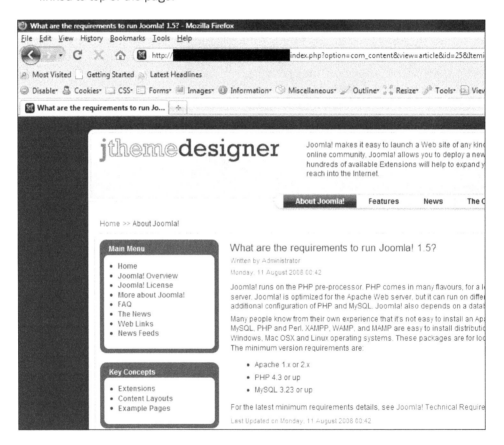

2. From the toolbar in Firefox, select **Tools | Web Developer | CSS | Display CSS By Media Type | Print**.

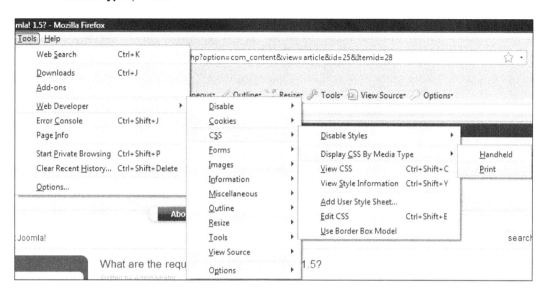

3. You will now see the page as it would be seen with the print stylesheet applied:

Joomla! makes it easy to launch a Web site of any kind. Whether you want a brochure site or you are building a large online community, Joomla! allows you to deploy a new site in minutes and add extra functionality as you need it. The hundreds of available Extensions will help to expand your site and allow you to deliver new services that extend your reach into the Internet.

- About Joomla!
- Features
- News
- The Community

search...

Home » About Joomla!

Main Menu

- Home
- Joomla! Overview
- Joomla! License
- More about Joomla!
  - FAQ
  - The News
  - Web Links
  - News Feeds

Key Concepts

- Extensions
- Content Layouts
- Example Pages

What are the requirements to run Joomla! 1.5?

Written by Administrator

Monday, 11 August 2008 00:42

Joomla! runs on the PHP pre-processor. PHP comes in many flavours, for a lot of operating systems. Beside PHP you will need a Web server. Joomla! is optimized for the Apache Web server, but it can run on different Web servers like Microsoft IIS it just requires additional configuration of PHP and MySQL. Joomla! also depends on a database, for this currently you can only use MySQL.

Many people know from their own experience that it's not easy to install an Apache Web server and it gets harder if you want to add MySQL, PHP and Perl. XAMPP, WAMP, and MAMP are easy to install distributions containing Apache, MySQL, PHP and Perl for the Windows, Mac OSX and Linux operating systems. These packages are for localhost installations on non-public servers only.

The minimum version requirements are:

- Apache 1.x or 2.x
- PHP 4.3 or up
- MySQL 3.23 or up

For the latest minimum requirements details, see Joomla! Technical Requirements.

Last Updated on Monday, 11 August 2008 00:42

 **Feed Your Brain with...** Books from the Joomla! Shop

Copyright © 2009 Joomla Themes Cookbook. All Rights Reserved.

Joomla! is Free Software released under the GNU/GPL License.

Powered by Joomla!, valid XHTML and CSS.

As you can see, the content is not nearly as well styled as the print pop up mentioned earlier, and there is a lot of unnecessary content still visible, such as the advertisement, navigation links, and the search feature.

See also

- ▶ *Styling links for print*
- ▶ *Typography for your Joomla! print stylesheet*

Adding a print stylesheet to Joomla!

The fundamental aspect of print stylesheets is linking them.

Getting ready

Open your template's `index.php` file and locate the content within the `<head>` section of the document.

How to do it...

1. Within the template's `index.php` file, add the following highlighted line within the `<head>` element:

    ```
    <head>

      <!—some code omitted -->

      <link rel="stylesheet" href="<?php echo $this->baseurl; ?>/
      templates/system/css/print.css;" type="text/css" media="print" />
    </head>
    ```

    This tells the template to insert a link to your print stylesheet. You should be able to see this HTML in your page once you've reuploaded the file:

    ```
    <link rel="stylesheet"
          href="/templates/rhuk_milkyway/css/print.css"
          type="text/css" media="print" />
    ```

The print stylesheet is now linked to your Joomla! template. We'll add to the print stylesheet in subsequent chapters.

How it works...

In many web browsers, when you view the print preview or print a page, the browser looks for a print stylesheet that is specified by the media attribute `print`, such as in our previous example.

See also

- ▸ *Styling links for print*
- ▸ *Preventing common bugs in print style*

Typography for your Joomla! print stylesheet

One of the most obvious aspects that we can change for our website's print stylesheet is the typography used. Although "sans-serif" fonts are typically easier to read on screen, it's often easier to read printed material in a "serif" font.

Getting ready

Open the `print.css` stylesheet that you created in an earlier recipe, located in the `templates\rhuk_milkyway\css\` directory of your Joomla! installation.

How to do it...

You can specify a **font stack** (that is, a hierarchy of type) that applies to your Joomla! template's print stylesheet with the `font-family` attribute in CSS:

```css
body {
background: #FFF;
color: #000;
font-family: "georgia", "times new roman", "times", serif;
font-size: 12pt;
}
```

It may also be a good idea to reset the `font-size` to a larger size for your print stylesheet to help legibility once the page has been printed. If you now view a page of your Joomla! website ready for print (for example, by using Firefox's Web Developer add-on), you can see that the typography has changed:

Yesterday all servers in the U.S. went out on strike in a bid to get more RAM and better CPUs. A spokes person said that the need for better RAM was due to some fool increasing the front-side bus speed. In future, buses will be told to slow down in residential motherboards.

- About Joomla!
- Features
- News
- The Community

search...

Home » About Joomla!

Main Menu

- Home
- Joomla! Overview
- Joomla! License
- More about Joomla!
  - FAQ
  - The News
  - Web Links
  - News Feeds

Key Concepts

- Extensions
- Content Layouts
- Example Pages

How it works...

By specifying the `font-family` attribute, we tell the browser which font to use when a page from your Joomla! website is printed. Defining the `font-size` helps to make sure that a browser's default values don't make your content too small to read once the page is printed.

Absolute font-sizes and print style

Although it is usually bad practice to specify a `font-size` in an absolute unit such as `pt` for screens, it's much more viable on paper as we're dealing with something that is of fixed-size—a piece of paper!

See also

▶ *Styling content for print*

▶ *Adding a print stylesheet to Joomla!*

Styling the layout of your Joomla! template for print

There are, as we have seen, quite a few elements of our Joomla! website that we do not need to be printed.

Getting ready

The elements that are not of use when we print a page include the search box, navigation links, the **Powered by Joomla!** footer, and advertisements.

How to do it...

1. You can hide the elements of the page, which are highlighted in the previous screenshot, by using CSS in the `print.css` file that you created earlier for your template.

```
#tabmenu,
#search,
.bannergroup,
.buttonheading,
. module_menu,
#power_by,
#syndicate
{
display: none;
}
```

2. You can now see a more suitable view for printing, which focuses upon the content in the page:

Joomla! 1.5 - 'Experience the Freedom'!. It has never been easier to create your own dynamic Web site. Manage all your content from the best CMS admin interface and in virtually any language you speak.

Home >> About Joomla!

What are the requirements to run Joomla! 1.5?

Written by Administrator

Monday, 11 August 2008 00:42

Joomla! runs on the PHP pre-processor. PHP comes in many flavours, for a lot of operating systems. Beside PHP you will need a Web server. Joomla! is optimized for the Apache Web server, but it can run on different Web servers like Microsoft IIS it just requires additional configuration of PHP and MySQL. Joomla! also depends on a database, for this currently you can only use MySQL.

Many people know from their own experience that it's not easy to install an Apache Web server and it gets harder if you want to add MySQL, PHP and Perl. XAMPP, WAMP, and MAMP are easy to install distributions containing Apache, MySQL, PHP and Perl for the Windows, Mac OSX and Linux operating systems. These packages are for localhost installations on non-public servers only. The minimum version requirements are:

- Apache 1.x or 2.x
- PHP 4.3 or up
- MySQL 3.23 or up

For the latest minimum requirements details, see Joomla! Technical Requirements.

Last Updated on Monday, 11 August 2008 00:42

Notice that the breadcrumb is still visible (**Home >> About Joomla!**). Breadcrumbs can be useful in orientating visitors who print content from your website, as it helps to identify a potential path they can follow through your website to find the content they printed online.

How it works...

By targeting specific areas of the website identified by `classes` and `ids` in CSS, we can specify what we want and what we do not want to be displayed when visitors view a page on our Joomla! website with the print stylesheet.

> **Finding the names of page elements for print CSS**
>
> The names of `classes` and `ids` may vary across Joomla! templates, but you can find the `classes` and `ids` that you require by looking at the source code of a page from your Joomla! website.

See also

- *Adding a print stylesheet to Joomla!*
- *Styling content for print*
- *Styling links for print*
- *Preventing common bugs in print style*

Styling content for print

The content is probably the reason your visitors are printing a page from your website, so it's worthwhile spending some time to style the content a little more.

Getting ready

Open the template's `print.css` file that you created in `templates\rhuk_milkyway\css\` in your preferred editor, which should contain your print style so far:

```
body {
background: #FFF;
color: #000;
font-family: "georgia", "times new roman", "times", serif;
font-size: 12pt;
}


/* Hide these elements from printing */
#tabmenu,
#search,
.bannergroup,
```

```
.buttonheading,
.module_menu,
#power_by,
#syndicate
{
display: none;
}
```

How to do it...

We now need to add more style to the print stylesheet to define styles for lists, headings, and other content.

- ▸ **Styling images**: It's a good idea to remove styling from images within your content for print styles, with the exception of a border surrounding the edge. The `float` attribute is set to `none` to prevent any problems with images wrapping content around in unsuitable ways when printing.

  ```
  img {
  border: 1px #666 solid;
  float: none
  }
  ```

- ▸ **Styling lists and paragraphs**: The next task is to apply some basic style to paragraphs and lists.

  ```
  p, ul, dl, ol {
  margin: 20px 0
  }

  ul {
  list-style-type: square inside
  }

  ol {
  list-style-type: decimal inside
  }
  ```

Our print style is beginning to look more defined:

The one thing about a Web site, it always changes! Joomla! makes it easy to add Articles, content, images, videos, and more. Site administrators can edit and manage content 'in-context' by clicking the 'Edit' link. Webmasters can also edit content through a graphical Control Panel that gives you complete control over your site.

Home ✉ About Joomla!

What are the requirements to run Joomla! 1.5?

Written by Administrator

Monday, 11 August 2008 00:42

Joomla! runs on the PHP pre-processor. PHP comes in many flavours, for a lot of operating systems. Beside PHP you will need a Web server. Joomla! is optimized for the Apache Web server, but it can run on different Web servers like Microsoft IIS it just requires additional configuration of PHP and MySQL. Joomla! also depends on a database, for this currently you can only use MySQL.

Many people know from their own experience that it's not easy to install an Apache Web server and it gets harder if you want to add MySQL, PHP and Perl. XAMPP, WAMP, and MAMP are easy to install distributions containing Apache, MySQL, PHP and Perl for the Windows, Mac OSX and Linux operating systems. These packages are for localhost installations on non-public servers only.
The minimum version requirements are:

- Apache 1.x or 2.x
- PHP 4.3 or up
- MySQL 3.23 or up

For the latest minimum requirements details, see Joomla! Technical Requirements.

Last Updated on Monday, 11 August 2008 00:42

As you can see, where content has been defined within the `<p>` elements rather than with line breaks (`<br>` or `<br />`), there is now more spacing between paragraphs.

▶ **Styling headings**: Headings within content also need differentiating from paragraphs. In the *rhuk_milkyway* template, headings are not defined within `<h1>` or `<h2>` elements, (as you might expect) but with a class applied to a table cell (`<td>`).

To style the primary heading in the page, we need to target our CSS to the `.contentheading` class in the *rhuk_milkyway* template. To keep the print style ready in case we update our template to a fully (X)HTML and CSS-based layout, we'll also style the `<h1>` element:

```
.contentheading, h1 {
font-size: 250%
}

h2 {
font-size: 200%
}
```

```
h3 {
font-size: 175%
}

h4 {
font-size: 150%
}

h5 {
font-size: 130%
}

h6 {
font-size: 120%
}

h4,h5,h6 {
font-weight: bold;
}
```

How it works...

The first three lines of the CSS for the content provide some spacing at the top and bottom of lists and paragraphs, which helps to make content easier to read once printed. The remaining CSS ensures that bullet points appear alongside items in unordered lists, and that a number is displayed alongside list items in ordered lists.

In the CSS that styles the headings within our page, we style the heading elements (`<h1>...<h6>`) because although they are not used by default in the *rhuk_milkyway* theme, they can be inserted into pages within Joomla! by using some of the rich-text editors available.

There's more...

1. To test the headings' style within your print document, simply edit a page within Joomla! by selecting the page from the administration panel, under **Content | Article Manager**. (You may want to create a test page to do this if your template is live on your website.)

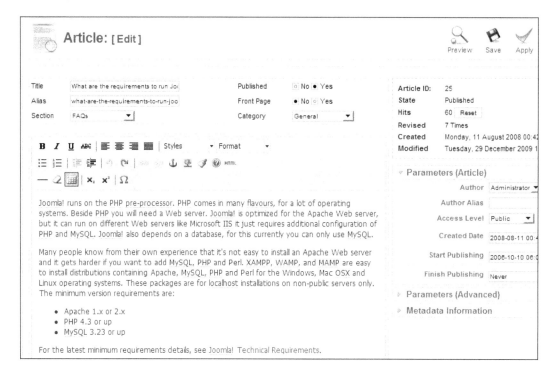

2. Add some test headings between blocks of content by selecting some text and choosing the relevant heading number from the **Format** drop down within the editor:

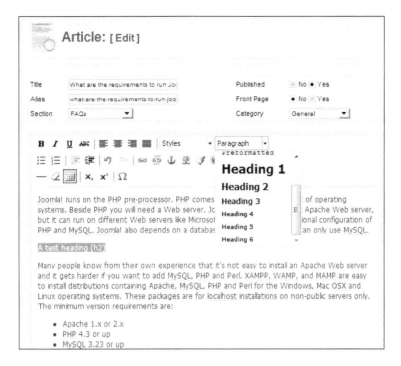

3. Once you've done this, you should see the style applied to the new heading within the editor:

4. If you view the page once you've clicked **Apply**, you'll see the new headings appear in the content:

What are the requirements to run Joomla! 1.5?

Written by Administrator
Monday, 11 August 2008 00:42

Joomla! runs on the PHP pre-processor. PHP comes in many flavours, for a lot of operating systems. Beside PHP you will need a Web server. Joomla! is optimized for the Apache Web server, but it can run on different Web servers like Microsoft IIS it just requires additional configuration of PHP and MySQL. Joomla! also depends on a database, for this currently you can only use MySQL.

A test heading (h2)

Many people know from their own experience that it's not easy to install an Apache Web server and it gets harder if you want to add MySQL, PHP and Perl.

A test heading (h3)

XAMPP, WAMP, and MAMP are easy to install distributions containing Apache, MySQL, PHP and Perl for the Windows, Mac OSX and Linux operating systems.

A test heading (h4)

These packages are for localhost installations on non-public servers only.

A test heading (h5)

The minimum version requirements are:

*   Apache 1.x or 2.x
*   PHP 4.3 or up
*   MySQL 3.23 or up

A test heading (h6)

---

5. View the page's print style again and you will see the style you assigned to each level of heading:

What are the requirements to run Joomla! 1.5?

Written by Administrator
Monday, 11 August 2008 00:42

Joomla! runs on the PHP pre-processor. PHP comes in many flavours, for a lot of operating systems. Beside PHP you will need a Web server. Joomla! is optimized for the Apache Web server, but it can run on different Web servers like Microsoft IIS it just requires additional configuration of PHP and MySQL. Joomla! also depends on a database, for this currently you can only use MySQL.

A test heading (h2)

Many people know from their own experience that it's not easy to install an Apache Web server and it gets harder if you want to add MySQL, PHP and Perl.

A test heading (h3)

XAMPP, WAMP, and MAMP are easy to install distributions containing Apache, MySQL, PHP and Perl for the Windows, Mac OSX and Linux operating systems.

A test heading (h4)

These packages are for localhost installations on non-public servers only.

A test heading (h5)

The minimum version requirements are:

- Apache 1.x or 2.x
- PHP 4.3 or up
- MySQL 3.23 or up

A test heading (h6)

See also

▶ *Styling the layout of your Joomla! template for print*

▶ *Starting your print stylesheet*

Styling links for print

Hyperlinks are fundamental in web pages, but they don't transfer so well to print.

Getting ready

Open the `print.css` file in the `templates\rhuk_milkyway\css` directory.

How to do it...

There are two aspects to styling links for print:

- **How the link itself appears within the printed version of the page**: It's a good idea to distinguish links that appear within content from normal text, as this can provide some context to the surrounding content. For example, it can tell a reader of the printed version that more information on a topic mentioned within the original article on the Web and recommended by the article's author was available.

  To this end, we'll use the following CSS in our print stylesheet:

  ```
  a, a:active, a:link, a:visited {
  font-weight: bold;
  text-decoration: underline
  }
  ```

- **How to get across the context of the link (the destination of the link) on paper**: Hyperlinks work on the Web because you're able to click (or otherwise select) the link and view the content on that linked document. When a web page is printed, you can't see where the link goes to. We are, however, able to append the address of the page that is linked after the link itself using CSS.

  ```
  a:link:after, a:visited:after {
  color: #333;
  content: " [" attr(href) "] ";
  }
  ```

Although the above won't work in older browsers, including Internet Explorer, it provides a good, unobtrusive benefit to visitors using more modern browsers.

> For the latest minimum requirements details, see **Joomla! Technical Requirements [http://www.joomla.org/about-joomla/technical-requirements.html]**.

How it works...

The `:after` CSS pseudo-element applied to links allows the address of the linked website (the `href` attribute of the link) to be placed into the web page after the text of the link.

See also

- ▸ *Styling the layout of your Joomla! template for print*
- ▸ *Adding a print stylesheet to Joomla!*

Preventing common bugs in print style

As with CSS for the screen, there are a few inconsistencies and bugs that appear in print stylesheets.

Getting ready

Open your template's print stylesheet; you'll be editing `templates\rhuk_milkyway\css\print.css`.

How to do it...

There are a few common bugs that you may come across when creating print stylesheets for your Joomla! website:

- ▸ **Firefox: Long, floated elements don't print.**

  Some older versions of Firefox will not print content within floated columns beyond the first page, where the floated column is longer than a page in length. The only way to prevent this is to specify `float: none` upon all floated elements within the print stylesheet.

- ▸ **Various browsers: CSS background image doesn't print.**

  A fairly common bug that occurs across a number of browsers is that background images defined with CSS do not print.

  If the background image is not relevant to the context of the article (that is, if it is just for decoration for your website's visitors viewing the content on their screen), this does not present a problem. However, if the image is required as part of the content, you should consider moving the image to within the content (by using the `<img />` element).

See also

▶ *Styling content for print*

▶ *Adding a print stylesheet to Joomla!*

6
Joomla! Admin Templates

Joomla! not only allows you to customize the pages that your visitors see but also allows you to customize the administration panel. In this chapter, we will look at:

- ▶ Understanding Joomla! administrator templates
- ▶ Installing a Joomla! administrator template
- ▶ Changing the administrator template
- ▶ Changing the logo in an administrator template
- ▶ Changing the colors in the administrator panel
- ▶ Securing the administrator URL
- ▶ Changing the icons on the Joomla! administrator dashboard
- ▶ Joomla! administrator template icon graphics

Introduction

If you use it on a daily basis, it can be a great idea to customize the look and feel of your Joomla! website's administration panel. It's also a useful task to do if you have clients or customers using the administrator feature of Joomla! and you'd like to customize the templates to match the identity of either your business, or your clients.

Understanding Joomla! administrator templates

Joomla! administrator templates are similar to the frontend templates for Joomla!. While frontend templates and associated files are located in the \templates directory of your Joomla! installation, administrator templates can be found in the \administrator\ templates directory.

Getting ready

View the directories and files in the \administrator directory. We'll take as an example the administrator template that is enabled by default in Joomla! 1.5, which is called *Khepri*.

How to do it...

As you can see, along with the familiar CSS, images, and JavaScript directories that are present in normal Joomla! templates, two new files, login.php and cpanel.php, are also present.

How it works...

Much like Joomla!'s frontend templates, Joomla! administrator templates have a hierarchy of related files such as stylesheets and images. Each administrator template requires an index.php file like a frontend template, but administrator templates also make use of a cpanel.php file that defines the administration dashboard, which is first displayed when you log in:

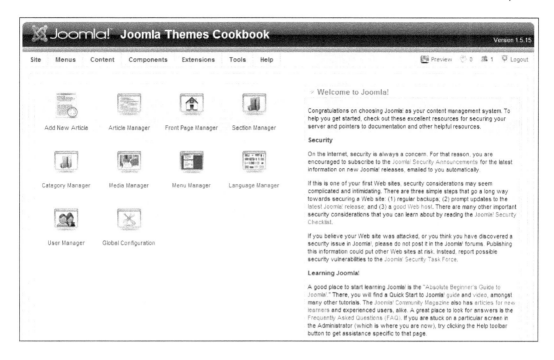

The control panel is defined in a separate file within the Joomla! administrator template as it allows for easier customization of the dashboard. You don't need to include a `cpanel.php` file in your Joomla! administrator template, but it's recommended to allow you to make the most of the screen when administrators first log into their website's control panel.

As with all Joomla! templates, the `templateDetails.xml` defines the files that are required within the template, as well as information about the template's author(s). Of particular interest in this file for administrator templates is the XML within the `<positions>` element:

```
<positions>
  <position>menu</position>
  <position>submenu</position>
  <position>toolbar</position>
  <position>title</position>
  <position>status</position>
  <position>icon</position>
  <position>cp_shell</position>
  <position>cpanel</position>
  <position>debug</position>
</positions>
```

Like frontend templates, Joomla! administrator templates rely on positions to insert relevant elements of the control panel into the template.

See also

▸ *Installing a Joomla! administrator template*

Installing a Joomla! administrator template

A fundamental task in changing your Joomla! administrator template is installing an administrator template.

Getting ready

You can find a number of free alternative administrator templates on the official Joomla! extensions website at `http://extensions.joomla.org`. Once you've found the administrator template you want to use, save it to your computer.

For this example, we'll use the *AdminPraise Lite* template, available at `http://www.adminpraise.com/joomla/admin-templates/free/adminpraise-lite.php`.

How to do it...

1. Log in to the administration panel of your Joomla! website, and go to **Extensions | Install/Uninstall**:

2. Next, select the template's compressed file from your computer and select **Upload File & Install**:

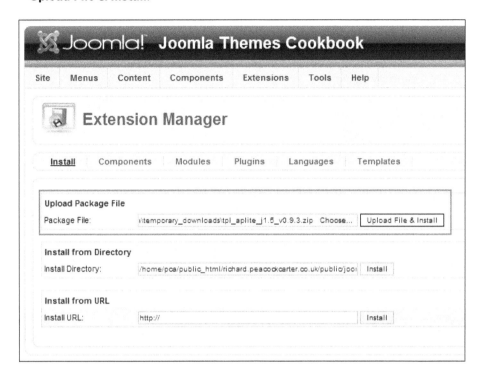

3 You should then see an **Install Template Success** message appear on the screen:

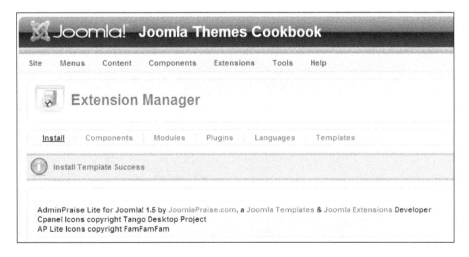

File permissions

If you receive an error at this stage, it's most likely because you need to set the directory permissions on the `\administrator` and `\tmp` directories to allow Joomla! to move and create directories. You will need to change the permissions on these files to allow **User**, **Group**, and **Public** access to the directory temporarily.

How it works...

The compressed file that you download has all of the files required for the Joomla! administrator template to function. Selecting it to install lets Joomla! decompress these files and store them in the `\administrator\templates` directory.

See also

> ▶ *Understanding Joomla! administrator templates*
> ▶ *Changing the administrator template*

Changing the administrator template

Once you've installed an administrator template, you'll need to enable it to see the new template.

Getting ready

Log in to your website's administrator panel and navigate to **Extensions | Template Manager**:

How to do it...

1. From there, select the **Administrator** option to view the administrator templates that you have currently installed.

2. Now you can see that we have two administrator templates currently installed—*Khepri*, which is currently enabled (it has a gold star beneath the **Default** column), and *APLite.*

3. To change the administrator template to your newly installed *APLite* template, select the radio button next to the template's name.

4. After that, all you need to do is click on the **Default** button at the top-right of your screen.

5. You've now changed the administrator template for your Joomla! website. The *APLite* template changes your administration panel to look like this:

How it works...

By changing the administrator template in Joomla!, you can instantly change the look and feel of how you manage your Joomla! website.

See also

► *Installing a Joomla! administrator template*

Changing the logo in an administrator template

If you want to customize your Joomla! administrator template, one of the most noticeable elements that you can alter is the logo that is displayed.

Getting ready

Prepare the logo that you'd like to use in your administrator template. We'll use the one based on the logo for the example site we've started to change:

We'll be using the *APLite* template in this example, though you can easily apply this technique to any Joomla! administrator template.

How to do it...

1. Open the template's `index.php` file, and locate the following code:

```php
<div id="ap-logo">
<!--begin-->
<?php
if(file_exists($logoFile)) { ?>
<a href="<?php echo $url;?>administrator">
<img src="<?php echo $logoFile;?>" /></a>
<?php } else { ?>
<a href="<?php echo $url;?>administrator">
<?php echo $mainframe->getCfg( 'sitename' ) . " " . JText::_(
   'ADMIN' );?> </a>
<?php }?>
<!--end-->
</div>
```

2. Replace this to reference your new logo file, which you'll upload into the `administrator\templates\aplite\images` directory, and call `logo.png`:

```php
<div id="ap-logo">
<a href="<?php echo $url;?>administrator"><img src="/
administrator/templates/<?php echo  $this->template ?>/images/
logo.png" alt="Administrator logo" /></a>
</div>
```

3. If you now save and upload the `index.php` file, you should see the new logo appear in the top-left of the screen. If you can't see the logo immediately, try refreshing your page.

▶   _Changing the colors in the administration panel_

Changing the colors in the administration panel

After changing the logo, the next noticeable touch you can make is change the color scheme used in your Joomla! administrator panel.

Getting ready

Open your administrator template's `general.css` file in preparation for editing it (we'll be using the _Khepri_ template in this example; other administrator templates tend to retain the use of `template.css` for the bulk of their style).

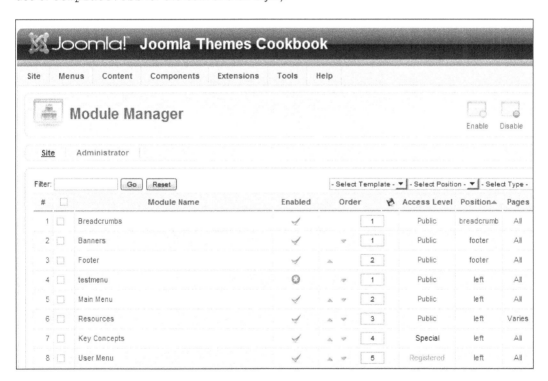

How to do it...

1. Our aim is to change the blue-colored elements used in this administrator template to match the green theme that we're using. In `general.css`, you need to locate the `.header` class to affect the color of the heading.

    ```
    div.header {
      font-size: 22px;
      font-weight: bold;
      color: #58962A;
      line-height: 48px;
      padding-left: 55px;
      background-repeat: no-repeat;
      margin-left: 10px;
    }
    ```

2. Next, style the other blue elements by doing a find and replace on `#0B55C4`, the RGB hex value for the blue used in the document, for your new green color, which is `#58962A`. In particular, you changed the colors affecting `table.toolbar a: hover`, which changes the style for the toolbar buttons to the top-right of the screen (**Enable**, **Disable**, **Save**, **Apply**, and so on), and the `h1` element:

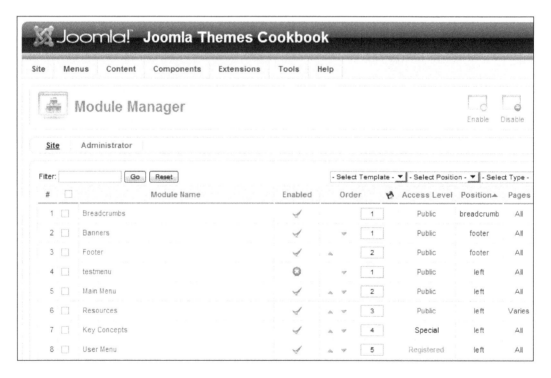

How it works...

By changing the stylesheets used by the administrator template, you can change the look and feel of your admin panel to varying degrees, allowing you to distinguish your Joomla! website from others.

There's more...

An alternative to changing the core files of the *Khepri* template is to create a copy of the template you want to change and make changes to that. This is done to prevent your changes being overwritten if you update the original *Khepri* template.

See also

- ▸ *Changing the logo in an administrator template*
- ▸ *Understanding Joomla! administrator templates*

Securing the administrator URL

One quite useful change you can make to your Joomla! administrator panel is to obscure the administrator login panel from view.

Getting ready

You need an extension called **jSecure Authentication** for this recipe, which you can download from the Joomla! extensions directory at `http://extensions.joomla.org/extensions/access-a-security/site-security/5809`:

jSecure Authentication POPULAR P

Version	1.0.9 *(last update on Jun 10, 2009)*		Rating ⭐⭐⭐⭐⭐		
Compatibility	1.5 NATIVE		Votes 271		Favoured 337
License	GPL	Type Non-Commercial	Views 151862		
Date Added	28 August 2008				

Developer Ajay Lulia   ⬇ DOWNLOAD   ⓘ SUPPORT
Website   Website

Drawback: Joomla has one drawback, any web user can easily know the site is created in Joomla! by typing the URL to access the administration area (i.e. www.site name.com/administration). This makes hackers hack the site easily once they crack id and password for Joomla!. Information: jSecure Authentication module prevents access to administration (back end) login page without appropriate access key.

The extension is free to download, but you need to register a user account to access the file.

How to do it...

1. Install the extension through the **Extensions | Install/Uninstall** option in your Joomla! administrator panel. In particular, you'll need to ensure that the \tmp and \plugins\system directories have the necessary permissions set to allow Joomla! to copy files to and from them. Next, you need to navigate to **Extensions | Plugin Manager**.

2. Enable the plugin, which can be found in the list of plugins under the name **System - jSecure Authentication**:

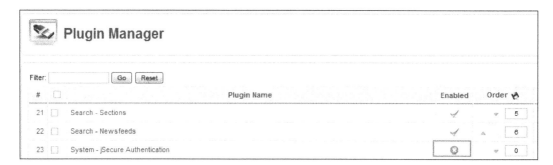

3. Once installed and configured, log out of your administrator panel and visit the administrator URL, for example, `example.com/administrator`. You'll see an error page rather than a login panel for your Joomla! administrator tool:

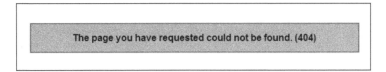

The page you have requested could not be found. (404)

4. If you now visit `example.com/administrator?jSecure`, you'll see the login panel:

The default keyword to access your administrator panel is **jSecure**. You can configure your keyword from the **Plugin Manager**—it's highly recommended that you change this as soon as the extension is installed to make it effective in securing your website.

[Remember that the keyword is case sensitive.]

How it works...

The extension helps to prevent unwanted visitors or users to the Joomla! administration panel by requiring an additional keyword appended to the end of the administrator panel's URL in the form of a parameter. Without this keyword at the end of the address, visitors will see an error page, which is by default set to be `joomla/plugins/system/404.html`.

See also

- *Changing the logo in an administrator template*
- *Understanding Joomla! administrator templates*

Changing the icons on the Joomla! administrator dashboard

You may wish to change the icons that are displayed on Joomla!'s administrator dashboard in the *Khepri* template, which is enabled as your administrator template by default.

Getting ready

Firstly, let's take a look at the Joomla! administrator dashboard, which is located by visiting the `\administrator` directory of your Joomla! installation in your browser. For example, if you have Joomla! installed at `http://www.example.com`, you access the administration panel at `http://www.example.com/administrator`.

So, the *Khepri* template looks like this:

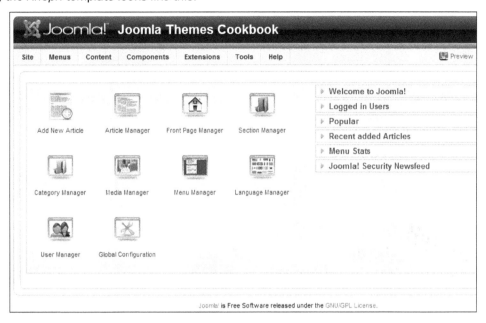

How to do it...

1. You will need to open the `mod_quickicon.php` file in the `\administrator\ modules\mod_quickicon\` directory of your Joomla! installation. Your aim is to change the **Add New Article** icon (highlighted below) to make it more obvious for a new administrator for your Joomla! website:

2. You now need to locate the line in `mod_quickicon.php` that reads as follows:

```
quickiconButton( $link, 'icon-48-article-add.png',
    JText::_( 'Add New Article' ) );
```

3. You can then change this filename to your **Add New Article** icon, which we'll call
   `icon-48-article-add_new.png`:

   ```
   quickiconButton( $link, 'icon-48-article-add_new.png',
     JText::_( 'Add New Article' ) );
   ```

4. Now you need to upload the new icon image for Joomla! to use in the
   `\administrator\templates\khepri\images\header` directory,
   assuming that you are using the *Khepri* Joomla! administrator template. Your
   new icon looks like this:

Joomla! administrator template icon graphics

To keep the look and feel of the Joomla! administrator panel consistent, it's best to use icons
that are sized to 48 x 48 pixels.

If you now refresh the administration panel's dashboard, you'll see the new icon appear:

How it works...

By changing the path to icon images in the `mod_quickicons.php` file, you can change the appearance of the icons in the administrator panel.

There's more...

As always, editing "core" Joomla! files (as in this case) may cause your changes to disappear when you upgrade to a newer version of Joomla!, so it's worthwhile maintaining a separate copy of all of the files you've just changed, just in case!

See also

- *Changing the logo in an administrator template*
- *Understanding Joomla! administrator templates*

7
Social Media and Joomla!

With the increasing popularity of social media, it can be worth considering making use of social media tools to engage and interact with your Joomla! website's visitors. This chapter covers:

- ▸ Integrating Twitter with Joomla!
- ▸ Integrating AddThis social bookmarking tool with your Joomla! template
- ▸ Embedding YouTube and other videos in your Joomla! website
- ▸ Configuring the DisQus Comments extension for Joomla!
- ▸ Integrating Facebook into your Joomla! website

Introduction

Years ago, websites were simply brochures or articles designed to inform. They've since moved on to help businesses sell to customers across the world, and now visitors expect to be able to interact with websites, adding their own opinions and content, and sharing what they find with friends, colleagues, and relatives globally.

Integrating Twitter with Joomla!

Twitter (`http://twitter.com`) is a popular microblogging service with millions of users. The service allows users to update a status of just 140 characters.

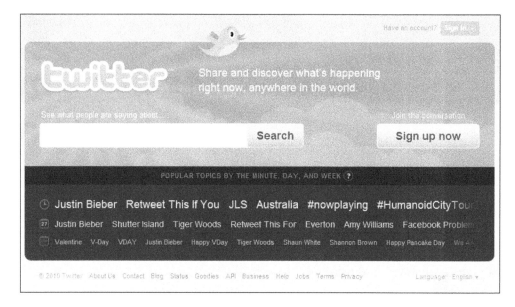

There are two potential uses of Twitter on your website:

- Displaying your most recent statuses from Twitter on your Joomla! website
- Tweeting new content added to your Joomla! website to a Twitter account

We'll concentrate on the first of these tasks.

Posting content updates to Twitter

If you want to post content updates that you make to your Joomla! website, try the **Twitter Status** extension, available from the official Joomla! extensions directory at `http://extensions.joomla.org/extensions/3735/details`.

Getting ready

1. Firstly, you need to download the **jTweet** extension from Joomla! Bamboo (`http://www.joomlabamboo.com/joomla-extensions/free-joomla-extensions/jtweet-free-joomla-twitter-module`).

2. Install the extension on your Joomla! website through the administration panel of your Joomla! website by navigating to **Extensions | Install/Uninstall**. Select the compressed file containing the extension, and then click on **Upload File & Install**:

3. You should then see the **Install Module Success** message:

How to do it...

1. You can now configure the jTweet extension from the **Extensions | Module Manager** section of the Joomla! administration panel. Your first task is to enable the extension by toggling the **Enabled** value for the **jTweet** extension.

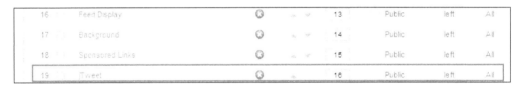

2. Once enabled, visit the frontend of your website (not the administration panel), and you will see that the extension is displayed in your template (the default template position of the module is "left").

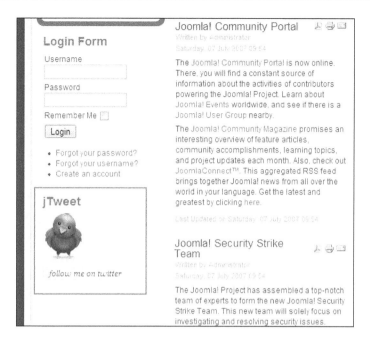

3. Return to the Joomla! administration panel, go to the **Plugins** option, and select **jTweet** from the list again to configure the jTweet extension. You need to:

   ❑ Change the title displayed in your template

   ❑ Tell the extension your Twitter account's username

4. To change the title of the extension displayed in the template, edit the value next to the **Title** label (to the left of the screen). We'll call it **My Tweets**:

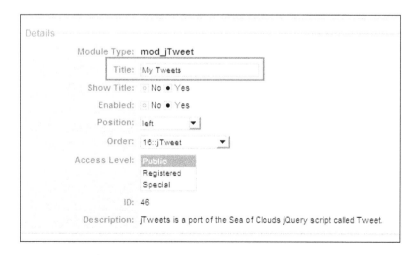

5. Next, provide the extension with your Twitter account username, located to the right of the screen:

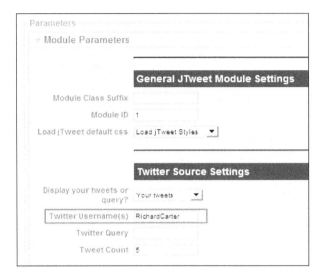

How it works...

The jTweet extension is based upon a jQuery extension for Twitter called **Tweet**, by Sea of Clouds, and is available at `http://tweet.seaofclouds.com`.

 As the extension relies on JavaScript, if a visitor to your website has JavaScript disabled, he/she will not see any tweets displayed.

There's more...

jTweet uses its own stylesheet to style the tweets on your Joomla! website. You'll find the stylesheet in the module's `\mod_jTweet\css\` directory; the file is called `jTweet.css`.

 Be sure to create a backup copy of the `jTweet.css` file before making any changes, in case you need to revert to the old version.

See also

▶ *Integrating AddThis social bookmarking tool with your Joomla! template*

▶ *Embedding YouTube and other videos in your Joomla! template*

Integrating AddThis social bookmarking tool with your Joomla! template

One way to help promote your website is with the use of social bookmarking tools such as Digg, Furl, Mister Wong, Facebook, and Delicious. These websites allow users to share links to interesting content on the Web and to bookmark them remotely with access from any number of computers they may use.

There are huge numbers of social bookmarking tools, and it could be very time-consuming to add the ability for your visitors to make use of each of these social bookmarking websites. **AddThis** (http://www.addthis.com/) provides support for around 50 of the most popular services.

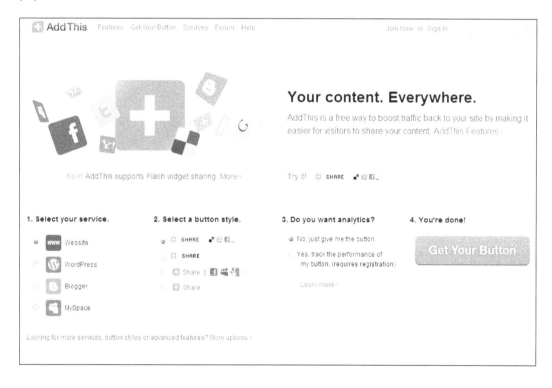

Getting ready

There are a number of extensions that allow you to add AddThis support into Joomla!
(see `http://www.addthis.com/tools/joomla`), but it's fairly simple to do so
without an extension.

1. Go to the AddThis website (`http://www.addthis.com`) and select the
   relevant options:

   ❑ For the **Select your service** option, select **Website**.

   ❑ Select your preferred style of button from the **Select a button
   style** option.

   ❑ For the **Do you want analytics?** section, choose between **Yes** or **No**
   depending on whether you want access to analytics for your button.

   ❑ Finally, select **Get Your Button**.

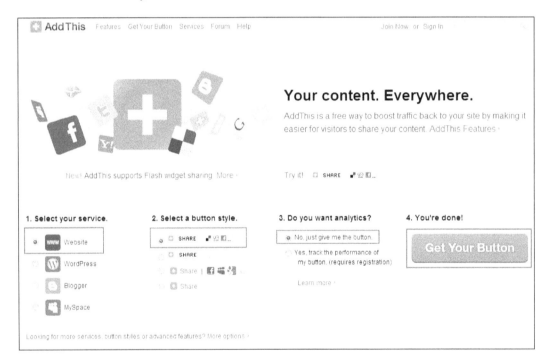

Registering an AddThis account

You can register an AddThis account, which allows access to statistics for
how your visitors are sharing your website. Although you are not required to
register an account to make use of AddThis on your website, you won't be able
to use the analytics feature without registering.

2. Once you've selected your options, AddThis will present you with the code that you can add to your Joomla! template.

How to do it...

1. Open your template's `index.php` file, and locate the content area, or wherever you want to include the AddThis button. In this example, include it under the page's content that uses the *rhuk_milkyway* template. Locate the following section of code in the template file:

```
<tr valign="top">
 <td>
  <jdoc:include type="component" />
  <jdoc:include type="modules" name="footer" style="xhtml"/>
 </td>
```

2. As we want our AddThis button below the content of the page, we can simply insert the code created by AddThis below the `jdoc` statement:

```
<tr valign="top">
 <td>
  <jdoc:include type="component" />

  <!-- AddThis Button BEGIN -->
  <a class="addthis_button"
  href="http://www.addthis.com/bookmark.php?v=250&amp;
  username=YOURUSERID">
```

```
<img src="http://s7.addthis.com/static/btn/v2/lg-share-
en.gif" width="125" height="16" alt="Bookmark and Share"
style="border:0"/></a>
<script type="text/javascript" src="http://s7.addthis.com/
js/250/addthis_widget.js#username=YOURUSERID">
</script>
<!-- AddThis Button END -->

<jdoc:include type="modules" name="footer" style="xhtml"/>
</td>
```

3. You will need to replace YOURUSERID in the preceding code with your own AddThis identity.

> You can move the `<script>` element to just above the `</body>` tag in your template's file: browsers will stop loading the page to deal with the `<script>` element, which can make the page appear to load more slowly for your visitors.

4. You should be now able to see the AddThis button appear on your Joomla! website once you've uploaded the `index.php` file and refreshed the page.

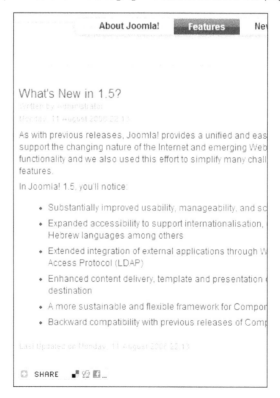

How it works...

AddThis takes the name of the page and its URL, and passes these into the parameters required by social bookmarking tools such as Digg, Facebook, Delicious, and Furl. For example, a Delicious to bookmark the page `http://www.example.com` looks like this: `http://del.icio.us/post?url=http://www.example.com&title=Title`.

Notice the `title` parameter (set to `Title` in the previous example), which allows us to pass the title of the page to Delicious too, adding this to the information Delicious stores about the page in its bookmark.

See also

▶ *Integrating Twitter with Joomla!*

▶ *Embedding YouTube and other videos in your Joomla! website*

Embedding YouTube and other videos in your Joomla! website

With faster Internet connections, video has become a large part of the Internet's content; news, articles, and opinions are all making their way into video. You can customize your Joomla! templates to allow videos from Vimeo, YouTube, and other video streaming websites.

Getting ready

1. Download the **AllVideos** extension from Joomla!'s official extensions directory at `http://extensions.joomla.org/extensions/multimedia/video-players-a-gallery/812`.

Save the compressed file on your computer and install it from the **Extensions | Install/Uninstall** option. Once installed, you'll see the **Install Plugin Success** message and information about the AllVideos extension. The most common problem preventing extensions from installing is incorrect file permissions, particularly on the \tmp directory of your Joomla! installation.

How to do it...

1. Once you have installed the extension, enable it from Joomla!'s **Plugin Manager** feature in the administration panel.

2. At the moment, an embedded video on your website looks like this:

Let's customize the look and feel of the embedded videos for the AllVideos extension.

3. Firstly, you need to copy the template files from the plugin's directory, which can be found at `plugins\content\jw_allvideos\tmpl`. Then, add them to your template's `html` directory; in this case, you'll be copying them to the `templates\rhuk_milkyway\html\jw_allvideos` directory.

 It's worthwhile keeping a copy of the original files at this point, in case you need to revert to them at a later date.

Of particular interest to us is the `template.css` stylesheet in the `templates\rhuk_milkyway\html\jw_allvideos\css\` directory. We want the area surrounding the video to be more consistent with our website, so we'll change its background color.

4. Locate the following piece of style:

```
span.avPlayerContainer span.avPlayerSubContainer {
display:block;
padding:12px;
margin:4px auto;
border:none;
background:#010101 url(../images/videoplayer-bg.gif) repeat-x
bottom;
text-align:right;
}
```

5. Alter the value for the `background` attribute to the purple used in your website's new logo, `#660080`:

```
background:#660080;
```

6. Now upload the `template.css` file back to your Joomla! installation's server and refresh the page, and you'll see the changes:

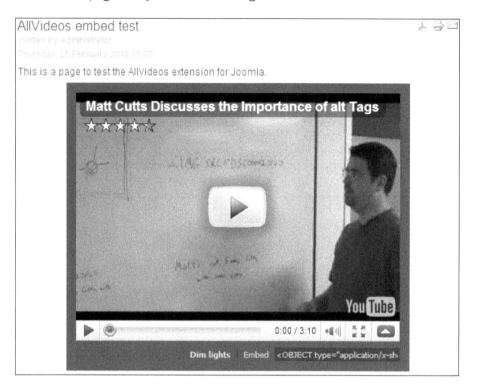

How it works...

The plugin allows you to use a simple format to insert videos into your Joomla!-powered website. The template files and stylesheets supplied with it mean you can easily change the plugin's appearance.

There's more...

Once you've installed the AllVideos extension, you can embed videos from websites such as YouTube by adding special tags in the following format:

```
{youtube}Ll7UFxqI2pM{/youtube}
```

Notice that the video's ID on YouTube is all that you need between the `{youtube}` tags. You can also embed MP3 and video files from your own site into a page with this extension in the following format (note the lack of a file extension here):

```
{mp3}anmp3file{/mp3}
```

A disadvantage of using a Joomla! plugin to generate media players in your website is that your website will be slower to load, as the plugin has to be loaded and executed each time a visitor visits a page. It's possible to get around this problem by using an add-on such as the **JCE Media Manager** feature (`http://www.joomlacontenteditor.net`). Note that you will need to buy a JCE license to use this, though.

See also

▸ *Integrating Twitter with Joomla!*

▸ *Integrating AddThis social bookmarking tool with your Joomla! template*

Configuring the DisQus Comments extension for Joomla!

Allowing your visitors to comment on your website is a good way to encourage a community for your website to grow and allows visitors to contribute their own thoughts to your content. **DisQus** (`http://disqus.com`) is a popular third-party comment management system that can be integrated with any content platform.

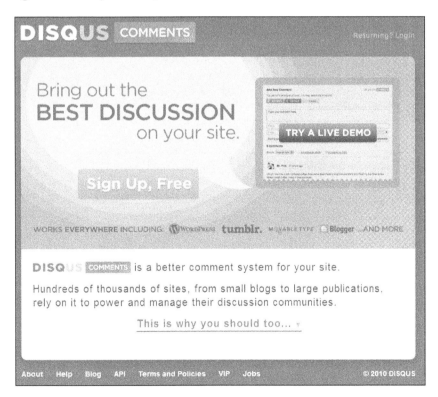

Getting ready

1. You will need to install the DisQus Comments extension for Joomla!, which is available from Joomla!'s official extension repository at `http://extensions.joomla.org/extensions/contacts-and-feedback/articles-comments/5259`:

2. Once installed, you should see the **Install Plugin Success** message and further information about the plugin.

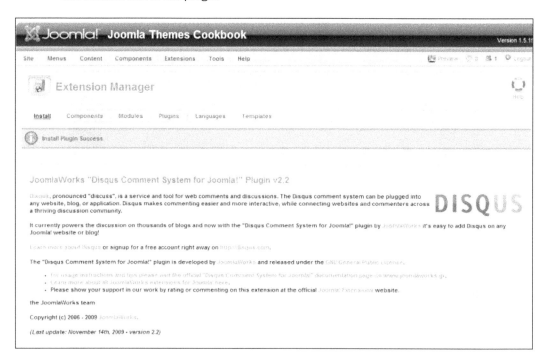

How to do it...

1. You can customize the appearance of this plugin (using template overrides) by moving the files located in the `\plugins\content\jw_disqus\tmp` directory to the `templates\rhuk_milkyway\html\jw_disqus` directory, where `rhuk_milkyway` is the name of your Joomla! template. Enable the plugin called **Disqus Comment System for Joomla! (by JoomlaWorks)** from the Joomla! administration panel's **Plugin Manager**.

Creating a Disqus account

You will need to create a (free) Disqus account in order to use this system. Sign up at `http://disqus.com` and return to this recipe once you have one!

2. Next, you'll need to enter your Disqus subdomain in the plugin's settings:

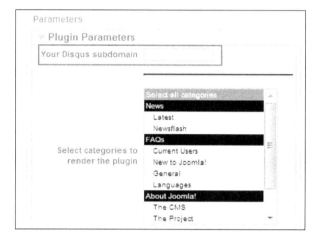

3. If you don't add your Disqus subdomain and attempt to load a page on the frontend of your Joomla! website, you'll see the following error message:

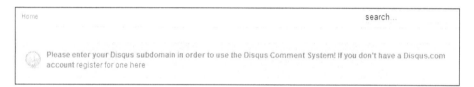

4. Once you've set up your Disqus account and have enabled the plugin, refresh a page to see the **Comments** feature appear. By default, Disqus adds a tally of the number of comments above the content of the page, and the ability to comment for your visitors beneath this content.

5. Open the `template.css` stylesheet, which is now located in the `templates\rhuk_milkyway\html\jw_disqus\css` directory. You'll change the colors to match your case study's color scheme more closely.

```
div.jwDisqusArticleCounter {
padding:4px 8px;
margin:4px 0;
border-top: 1px dotted #ccc;
border-bottom:1px dotted #ccc;
background: #F7D9FF;
text-align:right
}
```

6. Once the file's been reuploaded, you'll see the background color change to a pale pink, which is more in-keeping with your site's color scheme.

7. Next, you'll style the comments form itself by modifying the class `.jwDisqusForm`:

```
#disqus_thread {
padding:8px;
margin:8px 0;
background:#F7D9FF;
border:1px solid #ccc;
}
```

8. You can now see that the comment form has changed too:

How it works...

By overwriting the stylesheets provided by the plugin, you're able to define what the comments on your Joomla! website will look like to visitors.

See also

▶ *Integrating Twitter with Joomla!*

▶ *Integrating AddThis social bookmarking tool with your Joomla! template*

▶ *Embedding YouTube and other videos in your Joomla! template*

Integrating Facebook into your Joomla! website

Facebook (http://www.facebook.com) is another popular social networking website that allows you to befriend and send messages to other users, share photographs, and "like" pages representing everything from businesses to products and your favorite musical artists.

As a popular social tool, it is worth considering integrating Facebook with your Joomla! website. Luckily for us, a Joomla! extension exists that allows us to do just that.

Getting ready

1. Firstly, you need to download the **Facebook FanBox (LikeBox) Free** extension for Joomla! from http://extensions.joomla.org/extensions/social-web/facebook-display/9231.

2. Next, you need to download the extension (this requires registration, but it's free!).

3. You will also require a Facebook API key, which you can get from `http://www.facebook.com/developers`. If you haven't already, click on the **Allow Access** button that appears to confirm that you want to be able to get your Facebook API key. You will then see this screen appear:

4. Select the **Set Up New Application** button, seen to the right of the screen, and you'll be presented with the following screen:

5. Fill in the field **Application Name**; it's recommended that you use the name of your website here. Next, read the terms and conditions and select **Agree** (assuming you do!), and then click on **Create Application**.

6. You've now got your Facebook API key, located in the previous screenshot. Keep this value with you, as you'll need it later to get the extension you're installing to work.

How to do it...

1. Use Joomla!'s **Extension Manager** feature, found in **Extensions | Install/Uninstall** to install the file:

2. Select **Upload File & Install**, and Joomla! will install the extension on your installation. Next, you need to enable the extension. Select **Extensions | Module Manager** from the menu and type **facebook** in the **Filter** field. This will find the Facebook FanBox module.

3. Now, you need to enable the module by clicking on the red **X** under the **Enabled** column.

4. Next, you'll configure the module by clicking on the module's name to the left. When the next screen appears, look in the left-hand column for the **Position** value, and make sure that the extension will appear in a template position that exists within your template (we'll pick **left** here).

5. Next, look at the right-hand column under **Module Parameters.** You'll see a text field to add your Facebook **API Key** to, as well as a field for the Facebook **Page ID** of the page you want to link to your Joomla! website.

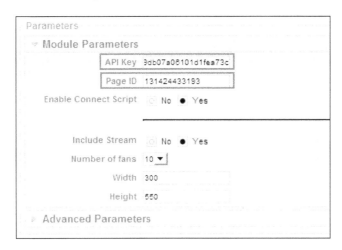

6. Your Facebook page ID can be found in the address bar of the page when you're viewing it (highlighted in the next screenshot).

7. Finally, you need to alter the width value so that your template can properly accommodate the Facebook content.

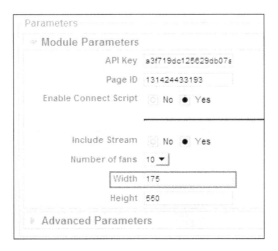

8. Click on the **Apply** button at the top-right of the screen to save these changes. If you now visit the frontend of your website by logging out of the administrator panel, you can see the Facebook extension at work!

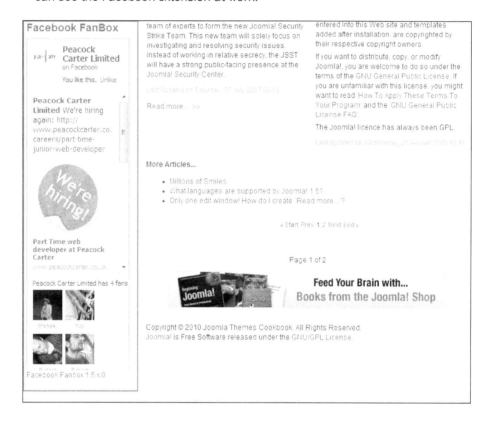

How it works...

The extension acts as a middleman between Facebook and Joomla!, allowing content from a Facebook page to be displayed as a Joomla! module.

See also

▸ *Integrating Twitter with Joomla!*

▸ *Integrating AddThis social bookmarking tool with your Joomla! template*

▸ *Embedding YouTube and other videos in your Joomla! template*

8
Styling Joomla! for Mobiles

In this chapter, we'll cover a range of topics to style our Joomla! website more effectively for mobile users:

- ▶ Adding an iPhone icon to your Joomla! website
- ▶ Specifying a handheld stylesheet for your Joomla! website
- ▶ Creating a mobile stylesheet for your Joomla! website
- ▶ Installing the MobileJoomla! extension

Introduction

With the increasing use of mobile and handheld devices to view websites, ensuring that your website can be viewed well on these devices is often a must.

Adding an iPhone icon

With the popularity of mobile phones and the use of the Internet on handheld devices, it can be worthwhile considering customizing your website to better allow mobile users to access your website.

Getting ready

Open your template's `index.php` file. You'll also need to create a graphic of 45 by 45 pixels to act as your icon.

How to do it...

Save the icon graphic as `apple-touch-icon.png` and upload it to the root directory of your Joomla! website. So, if Joomla! is installed at `example.com`, upload your file to `example.com/apple-touch-icon.png`.

How it works...

When displaying a website, an iPhone looks for the `<link>` element pointing to a suitable graphic for use as an icon, or a file called `apple-touch-icon.png` in the root directory of your website. This icon is then used on the iPhone's screen as a larger version of a favicon, should a visitor save a link to your website on their phone.

There's more...

There are a few options you have when creating an icon for iPhone users for your Joomla! website.

Precomposed iPhone icon

Firstly, the iPhone automatically rounds your graphic and adds the reflection effect across it to create the 'shiny icon' effect. If you'd prefer that your icon just appeared on your visitors' iPhone screen as you created it, simply name your file `apple-touch-icon-precomposed.png`.

Custom path for your iPhone icon

If you'd prefer to store your iPhone icon graphic in a different directory, you can use a `<link>` element defined in the `<head>` of your template's `index.php` file.

```
<link rel="apple-touch-icon"
      href="templates/rhuk_milkyway/iphone-icon.png" />
```

iPhone icon extension

There's also an extension available for managing your website's iPhone icon; it's called **iPhone Icon Plugin** and is available from the official Joomla! extensions directory at `http://extensions.joomla.org/extensions/core-enhancements/mobile/9521`.

See also

 ▶ *Specifying a separate stylesheet for mobile browsers*
 ▶ *Installing the MobileJoomla! extension*

Designing stylesheets for mobile devices

There are a number of common features that you can use across your styles for various mobile platforms.

Getting ready

If you don't have a mobile device to test your Joomla! template on, there are a number of online simulators for mobile browsers. One of the more popular mobile browsers is **Opera Mini** (http://www.operamini.com). The Opera Mini simulator is available online at http://www.opera.com/mobile/demo/.

Once you have read and accepted the **End User License Agreement** (**EULA**), you're free to type the address of your Joomla! website into the address bar provided.

 Note that you will need Java installed to use the Opera Mini simulator, which you can get at `http://www.java.com/en/download/index.jsp`.

How to do it...

There are a few factors that need considering when designing for mobile devices:

- The width of the screen is limited
- Mobile devices' support for certain elements we take for granted in web design for the screen are not necessarily supported

Screen width

The width of the screen is much smaller than the average screen for a PC or Mac; as such, multi-column layouts are not generally a good idea when presenting content to visitors on mobile devices. Common screen resolutions for mobile devices start at 128 by 160 pixels, and go up to 320 x 480 pixels and larger. As such, it's best to avoid declaring widths on any elements to allow the device to resize accordingly.

Limited support

Support for some elements can be limited. In particular, the iPhone does not support Flash elements in your website.

There's more...

The iPhone will attempt to adjust the size of your web page's text to better fit the screen; if you wish to disable this feature, you can do so with CSS in your stylesheet:

```
@media only screen and (max-device-width: 480px) {
 html {
  -webkit-text-size-adjust: none;
 }
}
```

The `@media` statement targets the iPhone (almost) exclusively, while the proprietary `-webkit-text-size-adjust` attribute targets solely WebKit-based browsers (in this case, Safari).

See also

▸ *Specifying a separate stylesheet for mobile browsers*

▸ *Adding an iPhone icon*

Specifying a separate stylesheet for mobile browsers

You can accommodate your website's visitors using mobile devices to view your website by specifying a separate mobile stylesheet.

Getting ready

Open your template's `index.php` file and locate the `<head>` section.

How to do it...

1. Insert the following HTML into the `<head>` element of the `index.php` file:

```
<head>

<!-- some code omitted -->

<link rel="stylesheet" href="<?php echo $this->baseurl ?>/
templates/rhuk_milkyway/css/handheld.css" type="text/css"
media="handheld" />

</head>
```

2. Once you have uploaded the file to your server, visitors on handheld devices should now see the style defined in your `handheld.css` file.

Testing your handheld stylesheet

If you want to view a simple approximation of what your website will look like on a mobile device, you can use Firefox's Web Developer add-on, available at `https://addons.mozilla.org/en-US/firefox/addon/60`. Alternatively, Opera Mini, a common mobile browser, has an online emulator at `http://www.opera.com/mini/demo/`.

How it works...

The link element tells browsers on handheld devices where to find a CSS file suitable for styling the content on your website for it.

See also

- ▸ *Adding an iPhone icon*
- ▸ *Creating a mobile stylesheet*

Creating a mobile stylesheet

Once you have specified a mobile stylesheet for your Joomla! template, you'll need to create a suitable mobile stylesheet. Things to remember when creating a mobile stylesheet are:

- ▸ Screen width is limited, so it's best to keep your website to a single column of content

- ▸ Large images and photographs will slow down the loading of your website for devices that may have a slower connection than most computers, and can be a barrier to your visitors reading content on your website

- ▸ Ensure the colors that you use are sufficiently different, as screen glare (for example, from the Sun) can mean that your design appears paler than on your computer monitor

Getting ready

Create a new CSS file in the `templates\rhuk_milkyway\css\` directory called `handheld.css`.

How to do it...

1. The style for handheld devices can be similar to the style for print; the aim is to minimize clutter and unnecessary content for each page. As such, you'll add this CSS to the `handheld.css` file that you created:

```
body {
background: #FFF;
color: #000;
font-family: "arial", "verdana", "helvetica", sans-serif;
font-size: 9pt;
}
```

```
/* Hide these elements from handheld devices */
#search, /* search */
.bannergroup, /* advert */
.buttonheading, /* page tools */
.module_menu, /* nav */
#power_by, /* footer */
#syndicate /* feeds */
{
display: none;
}
```

2. Now that you've defined a basic general style and hidden unnecessary areas of content, you can style the basic content elements such as paragraphs, headings, and images for your website.

```
img {
border: 1px #666 solid;
float: none;
max-width: 300px
}

p, ul, dl, ol {
margin: 20px 0
}
ul {
list-style-type: square inside
}

ol {
list-style-type: decimal inside
}

.contentheading, h1 {
font-size: 125%;
font-weight: bold
}

 h2 {
 font-size: 115%
 }

 h3 {
 font-size: 105%
 }
```

```
h4 {
color: #333;
font-size: 100%
}

h5 {
color: #666;
font-size: 100%
}

h6 {
font-size: 90%;
letter-spacing: 1px
}

h4,h5,h6 {
font-weight: bold;
}
```

3. Use Firefox's Web Developer toolbar to view the handheld stylesheet with the window width set to 320 pixels—a fairly common screen width for handheld devices.

How it works...

The `media` attribute tells handheld devices to load your `handheld.css` stylesheet rather than the default stylesheet that your Joomla! template uses.

Although the style that you've provided is very basic, it's more suitable for handheld devices and could be extended to create a design exclusively for handheld visitors to your website.

There's more...

It's also possible to specify your handheld CSS in your template's `template.css` file if you prefer, using the `@media` type definition:

```
@media handheld {
/* Your handheld CSS goes here */
}
```

It's better practice to separate stylesheets for different mediums though (as we did with the print stylesheet), as it means that only the minimal amount of CSS needs to be loaded for certain needs.

Hiding images that are too large for mobile screens

Another modification you can make to your Joomla! website's mobile stylesheet is to hide images that are obviously too wide for the screen. You can do this with the following code snippet:

```
@media only screen and (max-device-width: 480px) {
  img {
   -webkit-text-size-adjust: none;
  }
}
```

This doesn't prevent the device from downloading the image.

See also

- ▶ *Starting your print stylesheet*
- ▶ *Adding an iPhone icon*
- ▶ *Specifying a separate stylesheet for mobile browsers*

Installing the MobileJoomla! extension

In place of creating your own mobile styles for your Joomla! website, there is also a free extension that allows you to provide a mobile version of your website with minimal effort. The extension is called **MobileJoomla!** and caters for a wide range of mobile telephones with Internet access, from iPhones to BlackBerry devices and other smartphones.

As ever, the disadvantage of using a Joomla! extension to provide your visitors with a mobile stylesheet is that it adds to the page load time, as even if the extension is not used, it must be loaded.

Getting ready

1. Visit the MobileJoomla! website (`http://www.mobilejoomla.com`) to download the extension.

2. Select the **DOWNLOAD** button to the right of the screen and save the compressed file containing the extension to your computer.

How to do it...

1. Log in to your Joomla! website's administration panel and select **Install/Uninstall** from the **Extensions** option in the navigation menu. From here, upload the extension's compressed file once you've selected the file, and then select **Upload File & Install**:

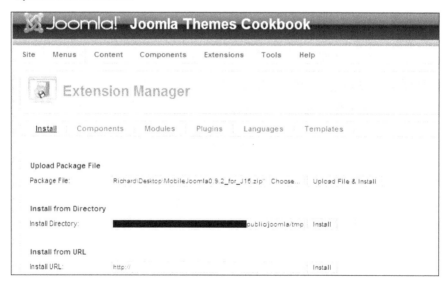

2. Note that the **Install Directory** setting should usually be set to the `joomla\tmp` directory. Once installed, you can configure the component to your website.

3. Ensure that the MobileJoomla! component is enabled in your Joomla! website's administration panel in **Extensions | Plugin Manager**; you'll find MobileJoomla! listed under **Mobile Joomla! Bot**.

Configuring the MobileJoomla! component

1. The settings for the MobileJoomla! component itself are accessible from the **Components | Kuneri Mobile Joomla! | Settings** option in the menu:

2. You'll then be presented with the **Global settings** pane:

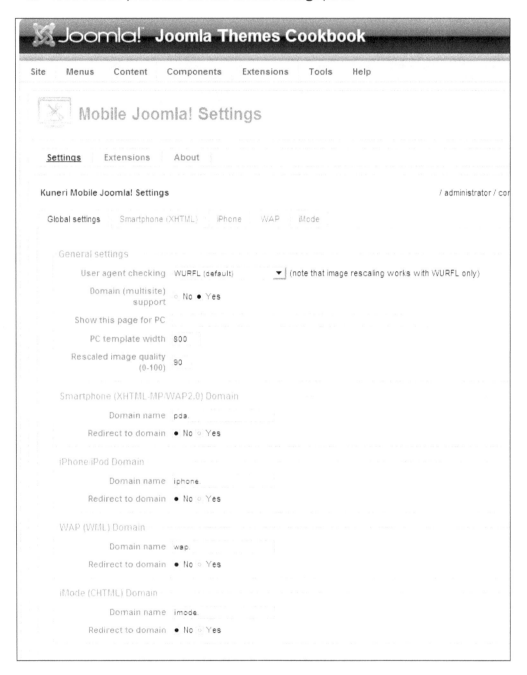

3. From here, you can set subdomains for each type of mobile version of your Joomla! website, from iPhones to WAP-enabled phones. One feature of MobileJoomla! that is of particular interest is the ability to set a custom Joomla! template per type of mobile device. As such, we'll demonstrate this for the iPhone; select the **iPhone** tab.

4. From here, you can specify a template for use on iPhone browsers for the **Template name** setting:

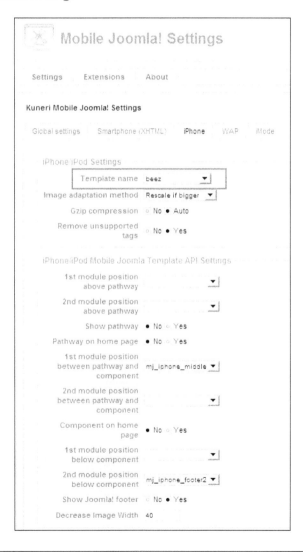

5. When you now visit your Joomla! website on an iPhone, you'll see the different template that you specified (**Beez**):

How it works...

The MobileJoomla! extension is able to detect a range of different mobile devices and provide the mobile device's browser with a different template, enabling you to totally change the appearance.

There's more...

If you just want to change your website's templates for visitors using iPhones, the **Auto Template Switcher** for iPhone is available from the official Joomla! extensions directory: `http://extensions.joomla.org/extensions/core-enhancements/mobile/5862`.

This option allows much heavier customization of your Joomla! website for specific handheld devices (such as the iPhone) than would be possible using CSS alone.

Further options

As can be seen in the previous screenshot, Mobile Joomla! offers quite a number of settings. Those that are of particular use to us are mentioned here:

▸ **Remove unsupported tags** allows Joomla! to strip out HTML elements that the iPhone does not support

▸ **Show pathway** puts a breadcrumb on pages

▸ **Pathway on homepage** gives you the option to remove the breadcrumb navigation from your home page if set to **No**

▸ **Decrease image width** allows images over a certain width (in pixels) to be resized especially for the iPhone

See also

▸ *Specifying a separate stylesheet for mobile browsers*

▸ *Adding an iPhone icon*

▸ *Designing stylesheets for mobile devices*

9
Joomla! and JavaScript

JavaScript can be used to a great effect to enhance your Joomla! website for visitors. This chapter includes the following topics:

- ► Including a JavaScript file in your Joomla! template
- ► Tips and tricks on minimizing page load time when using JavaScript
- ► Maximizing backward compatibility with JavaScript
- ► Providing Internet Explorer 6 with transparent PNG support in your Joomla! template
- ► Installing the jQuery JavaScript library in Joomla!
- ► Creating an image slideshow with JavaScript in Joomla!

Introduction

Joomla! is a feature-rich content management system, but there are some things it can't do out of the box. This is where JavaScript can become useful in improving the experience of your website to its visitors.

Including a JavaScript file in your Joomla! template

One of the most basic aspects of using JavaScript with your Joomla! template is including it within the page. There are two ways to do this—within the `<head>` element of your template, or within the `<body>` element of your template (best placed just above the `</body>` element). We'll make use of the method that uses the `<head>` template. (The reasons to do so are covered in another recipe of this chapter.)

Getting ready

Open your template's `index.php` template, located in your template's subdirectory within your Joomla! installation's `templates` directory.

How to do it...

1. Locate the `<head>` element of your Joomla! template in the `index.php` file and insert a `<script>` element that references the JavaScript file(s) that you wish to use:

```
<!-- some HTML omitted for brevity -->

<script
type="text/javascript"
src="<?php echo $this->baseurl ?>/templates/rhuk_milkyway/js/
javascript-file.js"></script>

</head>
```

Note that the base directory of your Joomla! installation is inserted automatically to help prevent any problems with changing directory paths to the JavaScript file, should you change your website's location.

 You will need to change the template's path if you choose to rename your template.

2. For valid XHTML, you need to specify the `type` attribute, as shown:

```
<script type="text/javascript"
    src="<?php echo $this->baseurl ?>/templates/rhuk_milkyway/js/
javascript-file.js">
</script>
```

How it works...

When a browser encounters a `<script>` element in your page, it loads the required behavior included in the JavaScript file, assuming that your browser has it enabled.

See also

▶ *Including a JavaScript file in your Joomla! template*

▶ *Maximizing backward compatibility with JavaScript*

▶ *Installing Google Analytics*

▶ *Integrating AddThis social bookmarking tool with your Joomla! template*

Tips and tricks for minimizing page load time when using JavaScript

While JavaScript can be used to enhance your visitors' experience of your Joomla! website, it can have a negative impact in terms of both real and envisaged loading times of pages.

JavaScript slows down the loading of a page because it's a *single-threaded* language. This means that nothing else can occur while JavaScript is being loaded or something in JavaScript is being evaluated. As such, a single, slow-loading JavaScript file can prevent a whole website from loading quickly!

How to do it...

1. The most obvious thing that you can do to make your Joomla! template load more efficiently is to compress any JavaScript you do use. As such, there are a number of online compression tools that you can use, including the **JavaScript Compressor** (http://javascriptcompressor.com):

2. Once you've inserted your JavaScript into the **Paste your code** input area, click on **Compress**. In this example, we've used a function that creates a slideshow with the use of the jQuery library:

```
// Requires jQuery to run

$(document).ready(function() {
        $('#slideshow-wrapper').cycle({
                fx:       'fade',
            speed:    'normal',
            timeout: 0,
            next:     '#next',
            prev:     '#prev'
        });

        $('#slidie').cycle({
            fx:       'fade'
        });
    });
```

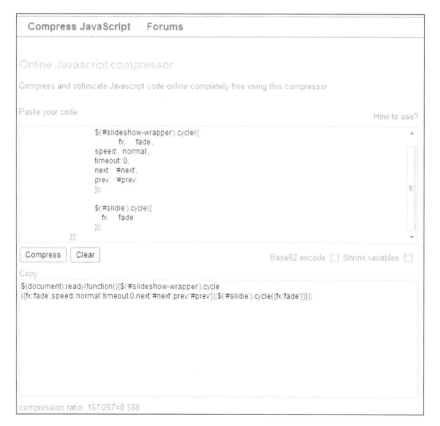

3. As you can see, quite a compression is noticeable even with a relatively compact piece of JavaScript, around half the size of the original in terms of memory required to store it (and thus, resources required to load it for a visitor visiting your website).

```
$(document).ready(function()
{$('#slideshow-wrapper').cycle({fx:'fade',speed:'normal',timeout:0
,next:'#next',prev:'#prev'});$('#slidie').cycle({fx:'fade'})});
```

Many JavaScript libraries (such as jQuery and MooTools) and features are available in a compressed format already. There is also a Joomla! extension called **JCH Optimize** that you can use. You can download it from `http://extensions.joomla.org/extensions/site-management/site-performance/12088`.

How it works...

As you've seen, JavaScript is a single-threaded language, so one technique to minimize its impact on your Joomla! website's loading times for visitors is to make the JavaScript the last possible item in the page to load. Additionally, compressing JavaScript can greatly reduce page-loading times with larger JavaScript files. It's also worth keeping a backup of the uncompressed JavaScript file, as this makes it easier to change and recompress in the future.

There's more...

Another way to minimize your Joomla! template's page load time is to reference JavaScript and other template files from different hostnames. Browsers including Internet Explorer and Firefox have been known to limit the number of simultaneous connections to a hostname, slowing down the loading of the page.

Moving <script> tags to the bottom of the page

The other major factor that can slow down the page load times for visitors to your Joomla! website is the necessity for their browser to have to stop while it deals with any JavaScript included in your page.

You can overcome this by reordering the HTML elements in your Joomla! template's `index.php` file to move the `<script>` elements to the bottom of the page where they appear inline.

See also

▶ _Maximizing backward compatibility with JavaScript_

▶ _Installing Google Analytics_

Maximizing backward compatibility with JavaScript

JavaScript can be used to get older browsers such as Internet Explorer 6 to behave like more modern browsers, to some extent. The `ie7-js.js` library uses JavaScript targeted at older versions of Internet Explorer to fix many of the common issues with these older versions of the browser.

Getting ready

As usual, you'll need to open your Joomla! template's `index.php` file and locate the `<head>` element.

How to do it...

1. Insert a conditional comment targeted at versions of Internet Explorer less than 7:

```
<head>

<!—some HTML omitted for brevity -->

<!--[if lt IE 7]>
<script src="http://ie7-js.googlecode.com/svn/version/2.1(beta3)/
IE7.js">
</script>
<![endif]-->

</head>
```

Note that the file is hosted externally from your Joomla! website on `googlecode.com`.

You may find a more recent version of the files you required link from at `http://code.google.com/p/ie7-js/`.

How it works...

The JavaScript changes Internet Explorer's behavior to allow its support for CSS as it would behave in later versions of the browser. Additionally, the `IE7-JS.js` file also provides a fix for the lack of transparent PNG support in the browser.

See also

▶ *Maximizing backward compatibility with JavaScript*

▶ *Providing Internet Explorer 6 with transparent PNG support in your Joomla! template*

Providing Internet Explorer 6 with transparent PNG support in your Joomla! template

One major letdown of older browsers is their lack of support for alpha-channel transparency in **Portable Network Graphics** (**PNGs**). This means that more modern designs may not display as intended in older browsers, but there is a fix in the form of the IE PNG fix.

Getting ready

1. Locate the `<head>` element of your Joomla! template's `index.php` file. You'll also need the **IE PNG Fix** behavior file, which you can find at `http://www.twinhelix.com/css/iepngfix/demo/`. Save this file in the `css` directory of your template's directory (use the *rhuk_milkyway* template in the following example).

   ```
   <!-- HTML omitted for brevity -->

   <style type="text/css">
   img, div, a, input { behavior: url(<?php echo $this->baseurl ?>/
   templates/rhuk_milkyway/css/iepngfix.htc) }
   </style>

   </head>
   ```

If you no longer have access to Internet Explorer 6, you could make use of a remote access service such as BrowserShots (`http://browsershots.org`). There's also a tool called **IETester** available online at `http://www.my-debugbar.com/wiki/IETester/HomePage` and `http://www.spoon.net` has a **Browser Sandbox** service available to allow for easier cross-browser testing.

2. Without the fix, Internet Explorer displays the transparency as a gray block around the image, as follows:

3. Once you've uploaded your Joomla! template's `index.php` file, Internet Explorer should now display the transparency as modern browsers do:

How it works...

Rather than displaying transparency, Internet Explorer 6 in particular displays a gray box in place of the transparency. The `.htc` file changes Internet Explorer's behavior to support the transparency.

There's more...

For more generalized support of Internet Explorer 6 in your Joomla! template, you can make use of `IE7-JS.js`, which is detailed in another recipe of this chapter.

See also

▶ *Maximizing backward compatibility with JavaScript*

▶ *Installing Google Analytics*

Installing the jQuery JavaScript library in Joomla!

There are a number of JavaScript libraries available that allow quicker development of JavaScript behavior for your website. We'll use the jQuery library, as this is one of the more popular JavaScript libraries.

Getting ready

Firstly, download jQuery from the jQuery website at `http://docs.jquery.com/Downloading_jQuery`.

How to do it...

1. Save the jQuery JavaScript file as `jquery.js` in the `templates\rhuk_milkyway\js\` directory. You may need to create the `js` directory yourself. Now open your template's `index.php` file and locate the `<head>` element within the template:

```
<head>
<!-- omitted content -->
<script type="text/javascript" src="<?php echo $this->baseurl ?>/
templates/rhuk_milkyway/js/jquery.js"></script>
</head>
```

That's it! Your Joomla! template now includes the jQuery library, meaning you can make use of it!

How it works...

There are many extensions to jQuery for specific features, from slideshows, container-toggling of contents, through to validating form input.

There's more...

Alternatively, you can install the jQuery library in your Joomla! template by editing your template's `index.php` file and placing a link to the library in the `<head>` element of your website:

```
<script type="text/javascript" src="http://ajax.googleapis.com/ajax/
libs/jquery/1.2.6/jquery.min.js">
</script>
```

jQuery from Google—an alternative

Another way you can include jQuery in your Joomla! template is by adding the following code to the `<head>` of your Joomla! template:

```
<head>
 <!-- omitted content -->
 <script type="text/javascript" src="http://www.google.com/jsapi">
 </script>
 <script>
  google.load("jquery", "1.4.2");
 </script>
</head>
```

This method of including jQuery allows you to configure which version of the library is loaded. The most recent stable release is currently 1.4.2.

See also

▶ *Creating an image slideshow with JavaScript in Joomla!*

▶ *Including a JavaScript file in your Joomla! template*

Creating an image slideshow with JavaScript in Joomla!

A common feature for many websites is an image slideshow that allows multiple images to be displayed in turn. Typically for Joomla!, there's an extension that provides this feature for us! The extension is called **Flash-Style jQuery Slideshow**.

Getting ready

Download the extension from `http://extensions.joomla.org/extensions/photos-a-images/images-slideshow/12135`.

How to do it...

1. Log in to your Joomla! website's administrator panel and navigate to **Extensions | Install/Uninstall**.

2. Select the extension from your computer in the **Upload Package File** field and click on **Upload File & Install**.

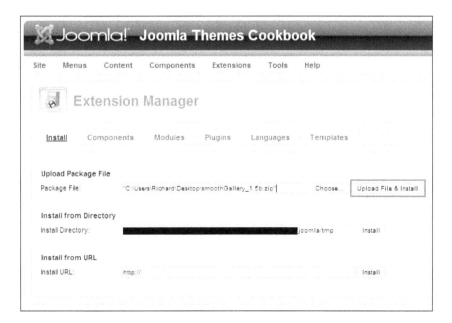

3. The extension is now installed! You can configure the extension by navigating to **Extensions | Module Manager**.

4. Locate the extension in the list (named as **Flash-Style jQuery Slideshow v2.0.2**) and enable it by clicking on the red cross icon to the right-hand side of the extension's name.

5. Next, configure the extension itself, moving it to display in the "top" module position of your template, and disable the title from displaying.

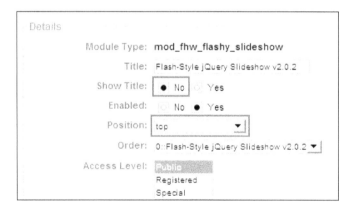

6. If you now look towards the right of this, there are more configuration options, as shown in the following screenshot:

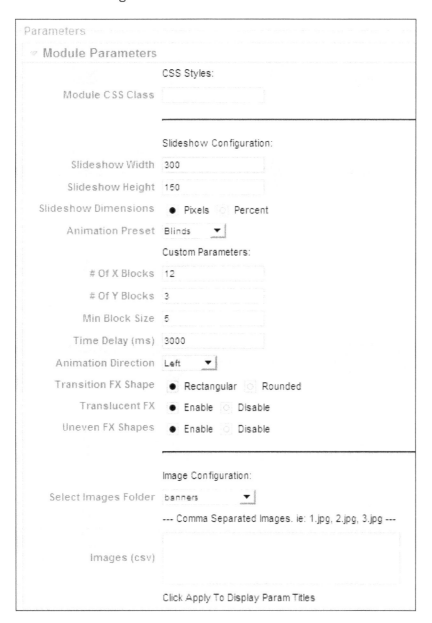

7. Add a class name to the **Module CSS Class** field to make it easier to style (if you wish to do so in the future). Once you've applied this change, the HTML generated for the module then becomes:

```
<div class="images-slideshow">
 <div id="fhwflashy58" class="fhwflashytrans">
  <img src="http://richard.peacockcarter.co.uk/joomla/images/
  banners/shop-ad.png"
  width="300" height="150" alt="" /><br />
 </div>
</div>
```

The path to the image itself will change depending on which directory of images you have selected for the **Select Images Folder** file. Lastly, you need to change the **Slideshow Height** and **Slideshow Width** fields to match the dimensions of the banner images. We'll be using **60** and **468** respectively.

8. If you now visit the frontend of your Joomla! website after saving these changes, you'll see that the images appear.

9. The image will change depending on the images you have in the directory you set earlier.

How it works...

The extension allows you to add a slideshow of images to your Joomla! website. JavaScript is then used to add a transition between the different images displayed in rotation.

See also

▶ *Including a JavaScript file in your Joomla! template*

▶ *Installing the jQuery JavaScript library in Joomla!*

10
Miscellaneous Joomla! Templating

This chapter covers a range of miscellaneous tips, tricks, and tasks to help get your Joomla! one step closer to perfection, including:

- Comparing your template across different browsers
- Validating your template's (X)HTML
- Validating your template's CSS
- Using conditional stylesheets in Joomla!
- Fixing the double-margin bug (in Internet Explorer) in Joomla!
- Installing Google Analytics

Introduction

A website is never truly finished: there is always content to add, pages to update, or designs to refresh. With ever-changing browser support and new bugs and discrepancies, cross-browser support can be the source of many headaches, and can be a large portion of the effort involved in maintaining a website.

Comparing your template across different browsers

Given the seemingly endless number of versions of browsers, getting your design to work cross-browser can be a daunting task. There are a number of common bugs that can be fixed or prevented with relative ease, and they are presented in the following sections.

Getting ready

Consider using a remote access service to test your Joomla! template cross-browser—**BrowserCam** and **BrowserShots** are two options. They provide a more convenient approach to cross-browser testing than installing every browser version on your computer!

BrowserCam

BrowserCam (`http://www.browsercam.com`) is a cross-browser compatibility testing tool.

BrowserCam is a paid-for service, though you may be able to access a free 24 hour trial.

BrowserShots

BrowserShots (`http://www.browsershots.org`) provides a service similar to that of BrowserCam, free of charge.

How to do it...

Simply enter the URL of your Joomla! website into the text field and wait for your screenshots to be provided. Once you're aware of a problem in a particular browser, you can go about fixing it with conditional stylesheets (for Internet Explorer), or otherwise.

How it works...

As different browsers use different techniques to display what you see on the page, there can be discrepancies between what one browser and another will display. The services mentioned above use a range of computers running different browser versions on different operating systems (Windows, Mac, and so on) to provide screenshots of how your Joomla! template displays in each browser.

See also

▸ *Fixing the double-margin bug (in Internet Explorer) in Joomla!*
▸ *Validating your template's (X)HTML*

Validating your template's (X)HTML

Validating your Joomla! template's XHTML can be a time-saver when it comes to debugging problems with your design's display in different browsers. Although pre-existing Joomla! templates may well contain errors in their HTML, if you're creating your own template you may find it useful to find errors in your Joomla! template.

Getting ready

Rather than visiting the W3C validator directly, some browsers provide tools to allow you to validate pages more conveniently. The **W3C** acts as the primary organization in creating standards for the website, such as CSS, XHTML, and HTML.

Opera (`http://www.opera.com`) has an option to validate the current page when you right-click:

The Web Developer add-on (`https://addons.mozilla.org/en-US/firefox/addon/60`) provides a similar feature for Firefox:

How to do it...

Most of the XHTML for your template is in the `index.php` file, and as such you can expect a greater concentration of invalid HTML to occur in this file. Further generated HTML can be found in the `\html` directory of your template (if it has one). If your template doesn't have a `\html` directory, the relevant HTML for the component will be stored in the component's own `\html` directory.

How it works...

Validation is an important factor in template design for Joomla! as:

▶ It should reduce the number of inconsistencies across browsers when displaying your website.

▶ Validated pages should be *future-proof*, that is, they should still be functional in older and newer browsers.

▶ Validated pages should load more quickly than invalid pages; this is good not just for your visitors, but for search engines too.

See also

▸ *Fixing the double-margin bug (in Internet Explorer) in Joomla!*

▸ *Validating your template's CSS*

▸ *Understanding template overrides in your Joomla! template*

Validating your template's CSS

Validating CSS for Joomla! templates can be a difficult task, especially if your template involves parameters for altering the color scheme. For example, in the *rhuk_milkyway* template, there can be four, five, or more separate stylesheets to validate.

Validating your CSS can be useful to debug any problems with your Joomla! template's presentation.

Getting ready

Firefox's Web Developer add-on (`https://addons.mozilla.org/en-US/firefox/addon/60`) provides a convenient link to validate the current page's CSS:

How to do it...

When you validate a page on your Joomla! website, you'll see any errors found by the validator:

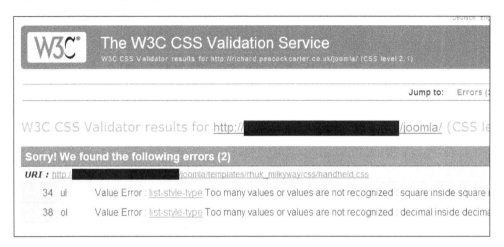

Where there are errors in more than one stylesheet, you'll see the errors categorized by their stylesheet to allow you to find the errors more easily.

How it works...

By ensuring your Joomla! template's CSS validates, you can help to prevent bugs or inconsistencies across browsers.

See also

- ▸ *Fixing the double-margin bug (in Internet Explorer) in Joomla!*
- ▸ *Validating your template's (X)HTML*

Using conditional stylesheets in Joomla!

Internet Explorer supports conditional comments that can be used to target stylesheets specifically to versions of Internet Explorer; these are known as conditional stylesheets. **Conditional stylesheets** can be used to alter the appearance of elements of your Joomla! website in the Internet Explorer browser, and are particularly useful in providing quick fixes to your Joomla! template that occur only in Internet Explorer.

Getting ready

Open your template's `index.php` file, which is located in the `templates\rhuk_milkyway\` directory of your Joomla! installation.

How to do it...

1. Within the `<head>` element of the template, add the following code:

   ```
   <!--[if IE]>

   <link href="<?php echo $this->baseurl ?>/templates/<?php echo
   $this->template ?>/css/ieonly.css" rel="stylesheet" type="text/
   css" />

   <![endif]-->
   ```

2. You can now specify CSS solely for Internet Explorer in the `ieonly.css` file in the `templates\rhuk_milkyway\` directory.

   The first of the two PHP snippets, `<?php echo $this->baseurl ?>`, inserts a path to the root of your Joomla! installation. For example, if your Joomla! installation is in the `/joomla` directory on your domain, this inserts `/joomla/` into the `href` attribute. The second snippet inserts the internal name of the template into the `href` attribute. For example, if you were using the *rhuk_milkyway* template, this would insert `rhuk_milkyway` into the page.

3. Next, update your template's `templateDetails.xml` file to reference the file:

   ```
   <files>

     <!-- other referenced files -->

     <filename>css/ieonly.css</filename>
   </files>
   ```

How it works...

The conditional comments are enclosed in a typical HTML comment style (that is, `<!—comment here -->`). Other browsers will ignore this, but Internet Explorer checks for the special format you see above, and depending on the version of the browser, will apply any stylesheets, JavaScript files, or other elements that you include within the conditional comment.

There's more...

You can target specific versions of Internet Explorer by using parameters in the conditional comment. There are five operators that you can use to determine the version of Internet Explorer accessing the page:

- ▶ **Less than** (lt) matches all of the versions of Internet Explorer less than the given version
- ▶ **Less than or equal to** (lte) matches the given version of Internet Explorer or earlier versions
- ▶ **Equals** matches the exact version of Internet Explorer
- ▶ **Greater than or equal to** (gte) matches the exact version of Internet Explorer and above
- ▶ **Greater than** (gt) matches all of the versions of Internet Explorer greater than the given version

Examples of conditional comments for versions of Internet Explorer

- ▶ The following conditional comment targets all versions of Internet Explorer:

```
<!--[if IE]>

 <!—insert stylesheet here-->

<![endif]-->
```

- ▶ The next one targets every browser *except* Internet Explorer:

```
<!--[if !IE]>

 <!—insert stylesheet here-->

<![endif]-->
```

- ▶ To target an exact version of Internet Explorer (for example, version 6), you can use the following conditional comment:

```
<!--[if IE 6]>

 <!—insert stylesheet here-->

<![endif]-->
```

- To target an interim version of Internet Explorer (for example, version 5.5), use the following conditional comment:

```
<!--[if IE 5.5]>

  <!—insert stylesheet here-->

<![endif]-->
```

- To target versions 6 and lower of Internet Explorer, the next one can be helpful:

```
<!--[if lte IE 6]>

  <!—insert stylesheet here-->

<![endif]-->
```

- To target versions 7 and greater, use the following conditional comment:

```
<!--[if gte IE 7]>

  <!—insert stylesheet here-->

<![endif]-->
```

See also

- *Fixing the double-margin bug (in Internet Explorer) in Joomla!*
- *Validating your template's (X)HTML*
- *Validating your template's CSS*

Fixing the double-margin bug (in Internet Explorer) in Joomla!

Internet Explorer is a very popular browser, but can often cause headaches for template designers due to its prevalence with the commonly used float-based layouts. A common bug is known as the "double-margin" bug.

Getting ready

We can use conditional comments to create a stylesheet that affects Internet Explorer only by linking a stylesheet within a conditional comment in the `<head>` element of your template's `index.php` file:

```
<!--[if lte IE 7]>

<link href="<?php echo $this->baseurl ?>/templates/<?php echo $this->template ?>/css/ieonly.css" rel="stylesheet" type="text/css" />

<![endif]-->
```

As these bugs affect versions 7 and earlier of Internet Explorer, you can safely target those of the browser only. You need to add this new style into the `ieonly.css` file in your template's `\css` directory.

How to do it...

As we saw earlier, there are a number of common bugs in Internet Explorer.

Fixing the double-margin bug

Firstly, we'll deal with the double-margin bug. This occurs when two `<div>` tags floated alongside each other have margin applied to them. For example, take the following HTML and CSS:

```
<html>
 <head>
  <title>Double margin bug</title>
  <style type="text/css">
   div.div {
   border: 1px black solid;
   float: left;
   height: 200px;
   margin-left: 10px;
   width: 200px;
   }
  </style>
 </head>
 <body>
   <div class="div">
```

```
        </div>
        <div class="div">

        </div>
    </body>
</html>
```

In most browsers, this creates two columns with a 10 pixel-wide margin to the left:

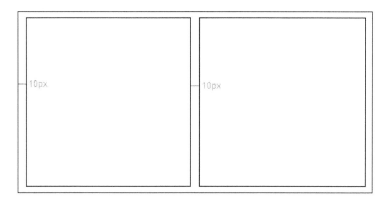

In Internet Explorer (versions 7 and lower), the first `div` displays a 20 pixel-wide margin to the left:

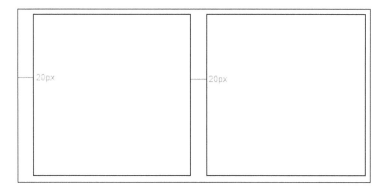

To fix this, all you need to do is add another attribute to the `div`. In fact, this needn't even go in your separate stylesheet, as it does not affect another browser's treatment of these elements:

```
<style type="text/css">
    div.div {
    border: 1px black solid;
    display: inline;
    float: left;
```

```
    height: 200px;
    margin-left: 10px;
    width: 200px;
    }
</style>
```

However, it is better for the loading time of your website to leave the conditional CSS within the separate stylesheet for Internet Explorer:

```
div.div {
    display: inline;
}
```

This causes the `<div>` tags to be displayed as intended:

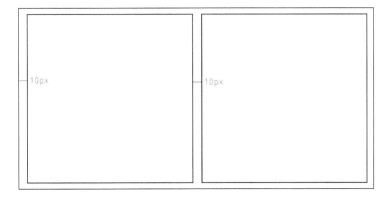

How it works...

The additional `display: inline` CSS solves the problem in Internet Explorer by enacting something called `hasLayout`, which changes how the browser 'draws' the content of the web page on to the screen. You can find more documentation about Internet Explorer bugs at `http://www.positioniseverything.net`.

See also

- ▶ *Validating your template's (X)HTML*
- ▶ *Validating your template's CSS*
- ▶ *Using conditional stylesheets in Joomla!*

Installing Google Analytics

Another common task that you may want to do with your Joomla! website is to track visitor statistics with the help of Google Analytics.

Getting ready

For this task, you'll need a Google Analytics account (which you can register for at `http://www.google.com/analytics`) and to retrieve the code provided once you have created a website profile.

How to do it...

1. Open your template's `index.php` file and find this code:

   ```
   </body>
   </html>
   ```

2. Before the `</body>` tag, add the code that Google Analytics provided for your Joomla! website. Once inserted, the bottom of your template's `index.php` file should look like this:

   ```
   <script src="http://www.google-analytics.com/urchin.js"
   type="text/javascript"></script>
   <script type="text/javascript">
   <!--// _uacct = "UA-123456-7";
   urchinTracker(); //-->
   </script>
   </body>
   </html>
   ```

 Note that the `UA-123456-7` value should contain your Google Analytics account reference, or else you won't receive your statistics!

How it works...

By including the Google Analytics code at the bottom of your template's `index.php` file, you'll be able to track your visitors' statistics on every page of your Joomla! website by logging into your Google Analytics account.

For more information on Google Analytics, see `http://www.google.com/analytics/features.html`.

There's more...

The above is a very simple way of integrating Google Analytics with your Joomla! website.

Google Analytics module for Joomla!

There is a Joomla! module that allows integration with Google Analytics, which you can find on the official Joomla! website: `http://extensions.joomla.org/extensions/site-management/site-analytics/1233/`.

See also

▶ _Understanding Joomla! templates_

Joomla! Output Overrides

This chapter goes into more detail about using output in Joomla! templates. Recipes in this chapter include:

- Customizing Joomla!'s home page with module output override
- Customizing Joomla!'s articles with component template overrides
- Creating a new module style (chrome) in Joomla!

Introduction

As you've seen throughout this book, there are a huge number of extensions for Joomla! that provide features you can add to your Joomla! website with little hassle.

By default, any HTML that these extensions provide is usually defined by the author of the extension in the extension's `\views` directory. Joomla!'s content component has its HTML defined within the `components\com_content\views` directory. This means that the HTML that is generated for say, the "article" type of content, is stored in `components\com_content\views\article\tmpl\` as `default.php`. To overwrite the way the HTML is output for this view, you can simply copy the `default.php` file from this directory to your own Joomla! template directory. For example, if *rhuk_milkyway* is the name of the Joomla! template that you're using, then you store your template override in the `templates\rhuk_milkyway\html\com_content\article\` directory as `default.php`.

Template overrides can be used to overwrite what Joomla! outputs at the module and component level. This means that you're able to customize Joomla! on a component basis (such as the "article" example mentioned earlier), as well as being able to customize what is output for modules (for example, a "latest news" block on your Joomla! website's home page).

Customizing Joomla!'s home page with module output override

Module overrides allow you to change what Joomla! outputs at a module level rather than a component level. This is what output is for the content surrounding a specific module, rather than around the component, which usually involves the entirety of a page.

In this recipe, you'll look at how you can use module overrides in Joomla! to change the **Latest News** module in the *rhuk_milkyway* Joomla! template. By default, this module appears on your home page towards the top-left of the main content block:

Getting ready

Copy the `default.php` file located in `\modules\mod_latestnews\tmpl\` to the `\templates\rhuk_milkyway\html\mod_latestnews\` directory. This file contains a mix of HTML and PHP that outputs the latest news on your website into the home page.

```php
<?php // no direct access
defined('_JEXEC') or die('Restricted access'); ?>
<ul class="latestnews<?php echo $params->get('moduleclass_sfx'); ?>">
 <?php foreach ($list as $item) :   ?>
  <li class="latestnews<?php echo $params->get('moduleclass_sfx');
   ?>">
  <a href="<?php echo $item->link; ?>"
   class="latestnews<?php echo $params->get('moduleclass_sfx');
   ?>"><?php echo $item->text; ?></a>
  </li>
 <?php endforeach; ?>
</ul>
```

How to do it...

1. Your aim is to add a clearer indication that the content is new, so change this to read:

```php
<?php // no direct access
defined('_JEXEC') or die('Restricted access'); ?>
<ul class="latestnews<?php echo $params->get('moduleclass_sfx');
?>">
 <?php foreach ($list as $item) :   ?>
  <li class="latestnews<?php echo $params->get('moduleclass_sfx');
  ?>">
   <a href="<?php echo $item->link; ?>"
   class="latestnews<?php echo $params->get('moduleclass_sfx');
   ?>"> <span class="new-content">New!</span> <?php echo
   $item->text; ?></a>
  </li>
  <?php endforeach; ?>
</ul>
```

2. Lastly, you'll add some style to your template's `template.css` file in the `\css` directory of your Joomla! template:

```css
span.new-content {
color: #C00;
font-size: 90%;
text-transform: uppercase
}
```

3. If you upload and refresh the page, you'll see your changes, as shown in the following screenshot:

Latest News

- NEW! Joomla! License Guidelines
- NEW! Content Layouts
- NEW! The Joomla! Community
- NEW! Welcome to Joomla!
- NEW! Newsflash 4

How it works...

Joomla! checks in the currently enabled template's `\html` directory for the HTML to output for a specific module, before looking in the module's default `\tmpl` directory.

There's more...

Overriding the module template means that you are affecting the content output by the Joomla! module. If you want to change the title or structure of the HTML surrounding the module content itself, you would need to change the module chrome (also known as module style).

See also

▸ *Customizing Joomla! articles with component template overrides*

▸ *Creating a new module style (chrome) in Joomla!*

Customizing Joomla! articles with component template overrides

You are not limited to customizing Joomla! templates at module level; you can define component template overrides to change what is seen for Joomla! pages of a particular type. Here, we'll look at customizing article pages in Joomla!, which, by default in the *rhuk_milkyway* template, looks similar to this:

We'll be customizing the template to add an automatic "mention this website on Twitter" graphic alongside the icons for viewing a PDF of the page, printing the page, and sending it to a friend via e-mail.

Getting ready

As articles in Joomla! are classified as part of the content component, the default template for articles is located in the following directory: `\components\com_content\views\article\tmpl\`. As usual, the file that you need here is called `default.php`. Copy this into your template's `\html\com_content\article\` directory.

You'll also need to save a Twitter icon with dimensions of 16 by 16 pixels in the `\images\M_images\` directory of your Joomla! installation as `twitter_button.png`.

How to do it...

1. In your template's `default.php`, which you copied above, find the lines that read:

```php
<?php if ($this->params->get('show_pdf_icon')) : ?>
 <td align="right" width="100%" class="buttonheading">
  <?php echo JHTML::_('icon.pdf',  $this->article, $this->params,
                     $this->access); ?>
 </td>
<?php endif; ?>
```

2. Below this, you can add the following code to create your Twitter button:

```php
<td align="right" width="100%" class="buttonheading">
 <a href="http://twitter.com?status=is reading <?php echo $this-
>baseurl ?>" title="Tweet this website">
  <img src="<?php echo $this->baseurl ?>/images/M_images/twitter_
button.png" alt="Post this to Twitter">
 </a>
</td>
```

3. Now visit an article page on your Joomla! website and refresh the page. You should see the changes that you just made take effect:

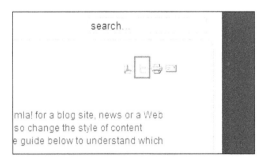

How it works...

Component template overrides work in a manner similar to that of module template overrides—Joomla! first looks in the currently enabled template's \html directory for a customized template for the component it is loading before resorting to the default template provided in the \components directory of your Joomla! website.

By adding ?status= followed by text to the end of the Twitter URL, that text is added to a Twitter user's status box, assuming that they're logged into their Twitter account. However, the text is not sent as a tweet to their followers until the Twitter user clicks on the **Tweet** button:

 Remember that Twitter can handle only 140 characters per message, so try and keep it short!

See also

▶ *Customizing Joomla!'s home page with module output override*

▶ *Creating a new module style (chrome) in Joomla!*

Creating a new module style (chrome) in Joomla!

Module styles, known as **chrome** in Joomla!, provide a way to change what Joomla! outputs into your page, on a module-by-module basis. Chrome in Joomla! templates effectively restyles the structure of the module(s) that is/are output into the page.

Getting ready

Module chrome is defined in Joomla! within the `modules.php` file in the `\templates\system\html\` directory. As usual, we want to avoid editing core Joomla! files (such as this one), so we will copy the `modules.php` file into our template's own `\html` directory in `\templates\rhuk_milkyway\html\modules.php`, assuming that we're using the *rhuk_milkyway* template.

How to do it...

1. To create a new module style for your Joomla! template, you need to add it to the bottom of the `modules.php` file that you just copied into your own template's directory:

```php
/*
 * Module style (chrome) that wraps the module in an unordered
list
 */
function modChrome_ullist($module, &$params, &$attribs)
{
?>
    <ul class="<?php echo $params->get('moduleclass_sfx'); ?>">
    <?php if ($module->showtitle != 0) : ?>
        <li class="title">
                <?php echo $module->title; ?>
        </li>
    <?php endif; ?>
        <li>
                <?php echo $module->content; ?>
        </li>
    </ul>
    <?php
}
?>
```

[Note that you gave the function a relevant name (`modChrome_ullist`). This is good practice, as it makes it more obvious to anyone else working on your Joomla! template what you're trying to do!]

2. If you now upload the `modules.php` file, your new module chrome will appear.

How it works...

By defining a new module chrome for our Joomla! template, we provide another option for the way the information in the page is structured with HTML. To define a new module chrome, we need three pieces of information (parameters) from Joomla!:

- The name of the module itself
- Any parameters associated with the module, such as the suffix value that is used to assign a CSS class to the `<ul>` element (`$params->get('moduleclass_sfx')`)
- Attributes of the module, in the previous case, this is the title (`$module->title`) and content (`$module->content`)

There's more...

1. To see your new module chrome in the frontend of your Joomla! website, you need to open your template's `index.php` file (as you're using the *rhuk_milkyway* template, this is found in the `\templates\rhuk_milkyway\` directory). Locate an instance of a `jdoc` statement in your template that makes use of the `style` attribute—a snippet of code that looks like this:

```
<jdoc:include
type="modules"
name="user1"
style="xhtml"
/>
```

2. You can change this to read:

```
<jdoc:include
type="modules"
name="user1"
style="ullist"
/>
```

3. Alternatively, you could add the following line, `code style="ullist"` into a `jdoc` statement if one doesn't already exist. If you now view the frontend of your website, you'll see a visual change to the user1 module:

- Latest News
  -
    - Joomla! License Guidelines
    - Content Layouts
    - The Joomla! Community
    - Welcome to Joomla!
    - Newsflash 4

4. There's also change behind the scenes in the HTML that is given. Previously, the HTML for this module looked like this:

```
<h3>Latest News</h3>
<ul class="latestnews">
 <li class="latestnews">
  <a href="(link omitted)" class="latestnews">Welcome to Joomla!
  </a>
 </li>
 <!-- other links omitted -->
</ul>
```

5. The new output HTML has changed structure:

```
<ul class="">
<li class="title">
Latest News
</li>
<li><ul class="latestnews">
 <li class="latestnews">
  <a href="(link omitted)" class="latestnews">Welcome to Joomla!
  </a>
 </li>
 <!-- other links omitted -->
</ul>
</li>
</ul>
```

See also

▶ *Customizing Joomla!'s home page with module output override*

Index

Thank you for buying
Joomla! 1.5 Templates Cookbook

About Packt Publishing

Packt, pronounced 'packed', published its first book "*Mastering phpMyAdmin for Effective MySQL Management*" in April 2004 and subsequently continued to specialize in publishing highly focused books on specific technologies and solutions.

Our books and publications share the experiences of your fellow IT professionals in adapting and customizing today's systems, applications, and frameworks. Our solution based books give you the knowledge and power to customize the software and technologies you're using to get the job done. Packt books are more specific and less general than the IT books you have seen in the past. Our unique business model allows us to bring you more focused information, giving you more of what you need to know, and less of what you don't.

Packt is a modern, yet unique publishing company, which focuses on producing quality, cutting-edge books for communities of developers, administrators, and newbies alike. For more information, please visit our website: www.packtpub.com.

About Packt Open Source

In 2010, Packt launched two new brands, Packt Open Source and Packt Enterprise, in order to continue its focus on specialization. This book is part of the Packt Open Source brand, home to books published on software built around Open Source licences, and offering information to anybody from advanced developers to budding web designers. The Open Source brand also runs Packt's Open Source Royalty Scheme, by which Packt gives a royalty to each Open Source project about whose software a book is sold.

Writing for Packt

We welcome all inquiries from people who are interested in authoring. Book proposals should be sent to author@packtpub.com. If your book idea is still at an early stage and you would like to discuss it first before writing a formal book proposal, contact us; one of our commissioning editors will get in touch with you.

We're not just looking for published authors; if you have strong technical skills but no writing experience, our experienced editors can help you develop a writing career, or simply get some additional reward for your expertise.

Joomla! 1.5 Template Design

ISBN: 978-1-847197-16-0   Paperback: 284 pages

Create your own professional-quality templates with this fast, friendly guide

1. Create Joomla! 1.5 Templates for your sites

2. Debug, validate, and package your templates

3. Tips for tweaking existing templates with Flash, extensions and JavaScript libraries

Joomla! 1.5 Development Cookbook

ISBN: 978-1-847198-14-3   Paperback: 360 pages

Building rigorously tested and bug-free Django applications

1. Simple but incredibly useful solutions to real world Joomla! 1.5 development problems

2. Rapidly extend the Joomla! core functionality to create new and exciting extension

3. Hands-on solutions that takes a practical approach to recipes - providing code samples that can easily be extracted

Please check **www.PacktPub.com** for information on our titles

Joomla! 1.5 Multimedia

ISBN: 978-1-847197-70-2   Paperback: 376 pages

Build media-rich Joomla! web sites by learning to embed and display Multimedia content

1. Build a livelier Joomla! site by adding videos, audios, images and more to your web content

2. Install, configure, and use popular Multimedia Extensions

3. Make your web site collaborate with external resources such as Twitter, YouTube, Google, and Flickr with the help of Joomla! extensions

4. Follow a step-by-step tutorial to create a feature-packed media-rich Joomla! site

Joomla! 1.5: Beginner's Guide

ISBN: 978-1-847199-90-4   Paperback: 340 pages

Build and maintain impressive user-friendly web sites the fast and easy way with Joomla! 1.5

1. Create a web site that meets real-life requirements by following the creation of an example site with the help of easy-to-follow steps and ample screenshots

2. Practice all the Joomla! skills from organizing your content to completely changing the site's looks and feel

3. Go beyond a typical Joomla! site to make the site meet your specific needs

4. Get to grips with inspiring examples and best practices and implement them to enhance your Joomla! site

Please check **www.PacktPub.com** for information on our titles

www.ingramcontent.com/pod-product-compliance
Lightning Source LLC
Chambersburg PA
CBHW060548060326
40690CB00017B/3638